Sisters-in-Law

Also by Nicholas Courtney

Shopping and Cooking in Europe
The Tiger
Diana, Princess of Wales
Royal Children
Prince Andrew
Sporting Royals
Diana, Princess of Fashion
Queen Elizabeth the Queen Mother
The Very Best of British
In Society: the Brideshead Years
Princess Anne
The Luxury Shopping Guide to London

Sisters-in-Law

A PALACE REVOLUTION

Nicholas Courtney

WEIDENFELD AND NICOLSON
London

For F.S.H.
with love

Published in Great Britain by
George Weidenfeld & Nicolson Limited
91 Clapham High Street
London SW4 7TA

ISBN 0 297 79291 1

Printed in Great Britain by
Butler & Tanner Ltd, Frome and London

Contents

Illustration Acknowledgements

The photographs in this book were kindly supplied by Syndication International, except for the following: Camera Press, 4 above; Tim Graham, 2 above; Lynn News and Advertiser, 1 left; Rex Features, 21 below.

Prologue

'Here is the stuff of which fairy tales are made,' began the Archbishop of Canterbury in his address to the Prince and Princess of Wales at their wedding. Here, indeed, was the *dénouement* of a real-life fairy story, publicly played out in its fullest and most exacting traditions of the genre: the handsome Prince, who, after years of searching, finds and marries his true love, a sweet and innocent bride, in a proper setting of glittering pageantry before a host of waving, loyal subjects and television cameras. It was as though the royal romance was needed by the British people not merely as innocent escapism, but to fulfil some deep-seated psychological need. As in the fairy-tale, the royal wedding was both pure fantasy and yet at the same time real, the epitome of what marriage is supposed to be about.

Having made the comparison, the Archbishop then felt it incumbent on himself to refute it, pointing out that whereas in fairy tales marriage is the perfunctory – 'they lived happily ever after' – resolution of a romantic search for courtship, for Christians the wedding day was 'where the adventure really begins.' However, despite his dismissal of that story-book analogy in the interest of dogma, Dr Runcie had made a sound observation, one of likening the Royal Family to the traditional fairy tale.

All legends, myths and fairy tales have their origins in reality. 'Some are born great, some achieve greatness, while others have greatness thrust upon 'em' is all the 'stuff of which fairy tales are made.' As a family, the Royal Family are obviously no different to any other family in the realm, although by nature of who they are, they are forced to be a much closer-knit unit than most. But, by being born Royal (born great), or becoming Royal through marriage (having greatness thrust upon 'em, except in the case of the Duchess of Windsor), and with the Sovereign at the head (achieving greatness), the Royal Family are indeed different. By the very fact that they are different means that they are automatically surrounded by an aura of mystique, a mystique that is so easily turned into myth, or fairy tale by the present-day storytellers, the media and biographers, mostly hagiographers. Like it or not, those members of the inner core of the Royal Family are *exactly* 'the stuff of which fairy tales are made.' The life-style and all the trappings have leapt straight from the pages of a fairy story – the princesses are beautiful, or are at least beautifully dressed, they live happily in castles and palaces, they are served by bewigged footmen and guarded by toy soldiers in scarlet tunics and bearskins; their loyal subjects sink to the floor in obeisance in their presence, the monarch bestows honours on the deserving, and so on. The comparisons are as endless as they are obvious, although many of the rituals and traditions owe their form to Queen Victoria and Prince Albert rather than to any ancient dynasty.

All good fairy tales thrive on repetition. The better known the story, the better it is loved; the more popular it becomes, the more it is wanted. Thus, royalness is a self-perpetuating myth that exists as long as the people have a use for it. With their riches and glamour, their lifestyle and power, the Royal Family can easily be (and indeed all too often are), mistaken for, or indeed confused with, the glitzy, American soap operas like *Dynasty* and *Dallas*. However, while in every episode of a soap opera something dramatic, preferably outrageous, has to happen to keep the audience continually gripped throughout the series, the protagonists of the fairy tale, the members of the Royal Family, have to do nothing but be themselves, and be thoroughly predictable, to sustain interest in their dynasty. Also, where the characterisation and deeds of the cast of the soap opera are created entirely by the director and script writer, the sympathy towards the Royal Family is left entirely to the individual, all of whom form their own opinions. However, apart from that outward show of glamour, riches and power, what this real-life fairy tale does have in common with the soap opera is that to both 'audiences' excepting the courtiers, the Palace coterie of friends, and those whom they meet on a regular basis, the protagonists are equally unreal, despite modern satellite television and state-of-the-art technology that makes it possible to beam the happenings of the Royal Family, live, to a giga-audience around the world.

This is the story of two girls, Their Royal Highnesses The Princess of Wales and the Duchess of York, who, in a decade of the 'upwardly mobile', have made it to the top of their particular tree; in the case of the Princess of Wales, to the very top. Their metamorphosis from commoner to royal, from ordinary girls (albeit with the right backgrounds and connections), to both real, and story-book princesses, was instant and, in all the right traditions of the fairy tale, dramatic. In marrying into that inner core of the revered Royal Family, they themselves have not only become royal, but taken on that 'mantle of royalty' and all that goes with it.

It would, of course, take more than the inclusion of a couple of commoners into the inner ranks of the Royal Family to radically alter the monarchy, but both the Princess of Wales and the Duchess of York are nonetheless flesh-and-blood young women of a certain class and background as well as a pair of vital characters fitting neatly into the existing fairy tale framework of the Royal Family. Each has her own prescribed role in the ritual, but as with every piece of fiction, the characters develop and change as the story unfolds. These real-life, nouveau Princesses are no exception. Their role and influence develop, not only in keeping with their own very different characters and backgrounds, but also in relation to the importance and seniority of their spouses. As in all fairy stories, the introduction of a commoner into the Royal Family does not dilute or weaken it — in fact quite the reverse where Queen Elizabeth the Queen Mother is concerned.

But 'to begin at the beginning' is to begin with the wedding. At least the Archbishop got that right.

The Weddings

It was hailed as the wedding of the century. And so it was
when, on 29 July 1981, His Royal Highness Charles Philip
Arthur George, Prince of the United Kingdom of Great
Britain and Northern Ireland, Prince of Wales and Earl of Chester,
Duke of Cornwall, Duke of Rothesay, Earl of Carrick and Baron
of Renfrew, Lord of the Isles and Great Steward of Scotland,
eldest son of Her Majesty the Queen and His Royal Highness
The Prince Philip, Duke of Edinburgh, married Lady Diana
Spencer, youngest daughter of Earl Spencer and the Honourable
Mrs Shand Kydd.

Of the dozens of royal weddings during the last hundred
years, none was as remotely as important as this, and it showed.
Technically, this was the first marriage in nearly a century of the
heir to the throne − when the Queen, as Princess Elizabeth,
married Prince Philip she was Heir *Presumptive*, even though it
was hardly likely that King George VI and Queen Elizabeth
would produce a son to take precedence over her. This royal
wedding was to be a peerless spectacle, a pageant commensurate
with the occasion that the British, in particular the Lord Chamberlain's Office, stage-manage so well. Then there were the bride
and groom themselves; she young and pretty, with a naivety and

charm that captivated the world. On the day, the weather – so unpredictable in England – held out. But above all and despite the hundreds of official guests – diplomats and dignitaries from so many nations, despite the pomp and circumstance – it was to be a family wedding, shared and enjoyed by millions around the world.

Although planned with equal care, the marriage of HRH The Prince Andrew, Duke of York to Miss Sarah Ferguson on 23 July 1986 was a less important affair. Barring the unthinkable, Prince Andrew will never become king, forever to be preceded by his elder brother and children. Nor was the wedding of a prince to a commoner particularly novel, Sarah Ferguson being just one of many to marry for love into the Royal Family over the last three or four generations. The supply of eligible royal spouses (or indeed the necessity to marry them) had been exhausted when monarchy became unfashionable in Europe after the First World War. Instead, this was just a fun, family wedding, gilded by the best in royal pageantry and enjoyed by the same, worldwide audience who had seen the Prince and Princess of Wales married with so much greater spectacle. The wedding was a much less formal affair. The extrovert style of this bride and groom was allowed to express itself, unrestrained by any constitutional role that either of them might, or might not, take on in the future.

It is just these small, but crucial, differences in the nature and style of those two royal weddings that symbolised the sisters'-in-law future lives and roles within the Royal Family: the Princess of Wales married not just as a wife but as a future queen, while the Duchess of York married a jolly, serving sailor who happened to be a prince.

As with all things royal, anything that happens more than once becomes a 'tradition'. In this century, it has become the 'tradition' that royal weddings take place in Westminster Abbey. However, for the wedding of the Prince of Wales and Lady Diana Spencer, it was their choice to break with that tradition for various practical and family reasons, not least that Lady Diana Spencer's acrimoniously divorced parents, the then Viscount and Viscountess Althorp, had married at Westminster Abbey. The memory of the funeral of the Prince's adored great uncle, Earl Mountbatten of Burma, just two years before at Westminster Abbey, must also have affected his decision. Instead, they chose St Paul's Cathedral for their wedding. Where Westminster Abbey can seat only 1500 guests, St Paul's can take two thousand more. Another advantage of St Paul's over Westminster was that it is three times the distance from Buckingham Palace, making a very much longer processional route which could accommodate more spectators. Apparently, when it was pointed out to the Prince of Wales when he chose the Cathedral that there were not enough troops to man the route, he dismissed it with, 'Well, stand them further apart.'[1] Also, St Paul's has the superior acoustics vital to both the Prince of Wales and Lady Diana Spencer's developed sense and love of music.

As with every family wedding, there are those family and friends that are really wanted, those who *ought* to be invited, and those who *have* to be asked. Lady Diana Spencer's guest list was comparatively easy with chosen friends, relatives and a few family retainers. Not so for the Prince of Wales for whom, as heir to the throne of Great Britain, Head of the Commonwealth and Defender of the Faith, there were hundreds of guests – a positive bran tub of monarchs, presidents, heads of state, politicians, diplomats, clerics and royal servants – that all *had* to be invited. Unlike Princess Margaret's wedding where the Dutch, Belgian, Swedish, Norwegian and Greek Royal Families all stayed away (they were peeved that their British cousins had not attended any of their major social events since the War), there were few refusals. However, the King of Spain boycotted the wedding over the plan to start their honeymoon from the politically sensitive Gibraltar, while the President of Greece objected to King Constantine, a family friend, being styled the King of the Hellenes. The Australian Prime Minister, Malcolm Fraser, stayed at home because of industrial chaos, while not many people minded that Ken Livingstone, leader of the Greater London Council, decided to boycott the wedding on political grounds, and the hugely corpulent, twenty-eight stone King of Tonga counted for two on his own, bringing his own, reinforced chair. St Paul's Cathedral took them all.

For their wedding, Prince Andrew and Sarah Ferguson revived that Royal 'tradition' in choosing Westminster Abbey for very much the same reasons as the Prince and Princess of Wales had rejected it. The Abbey being that much smaller was more intimate; for instance, as the seats all face inwards, as opposed to the rows of St Paul's, it made for a more 'cosy', family atmosphere. Although there were still those who *had* to be invited, like the Diplomatic Corps and members of the Government, there were far fewer of them, leaving more room for family and friends. For once, the Prime Minister, Mrs Thatcher, and the leaders of the opposition parties were barely noticed amongst the other guests, members of the Royal Family (with a sprinkling of foreign royals), and friends as diverse as the senior English Duke to 'show biz' stars like Billy Connolly and Pamela Stephenson, the Elton Johns, the Michael Caines, even Barry Humphries (significantly dressed as Edna Everage), the American comedienne, Joan Rivers, and David and Lady Carina Frost, who had a foot in both camps. The presence of these comedians and stars of stage and screen was a natural for the media. With the near total absence of the scarlet and gold, bemedalled, uniformed dignitaries so prominent at the Prince and Princess of Wales's wedding, these media personalities and close friends seemed to set the tone of a 'fun' wedding.

There was much criticism of the Prime Minister for not declaring a national holiday for Prince Andrew's wedding as had been done for his brother five years before. On this issue the Government could not win. They had been just as strongly criticised for the loss of industrial man hours when making the Prince of Wales's wedding a public holiday. Holiday or no, the crowds were equally enthusiastic, though not as great, for the Ferguson wedding as for the heir to the throne's. Some who had camped out all night, a few of whom had been there for many days, were rewarded by a glass of champagne sent out from Buckingham Palace.

There was that same genuine display of loyalty, patriotism and enthusiasm on both occasions, but undoubtedly the heir to the throne's wedding was seen to be closer to a coronation than a wedding. Although the *Spectator* was later to point out that a 'football supporter' element, clad in Union flags and painted red, white and blue, and chanting 'Lady Di, Lady Di, Lady Di', blurred the line between a joke patriot and a real patriot, the loyalty to the throne expressed at this wedding was less evident when it came to Prince Andrew's turn. Try as palace officials might, there was a touch of parody about Prince Andrew's wedding. Could this jokey couple seem other than flippant when set against the Prince and Princess of Wales?

For both weddings, the mood of the crowds was largely taken from the bridal couples themselves. With the comparatively serious Prince of Wales and his 'Dresden' bride, Lady Diana Spencer, the mood was one of great deference, overlaid with a sugary, dream-like romance. Even for Princess Anne's wedding, almost ten years before, there were mildly irreverent banners from good-natured well-wishers: 'It's too late to say neigh' signalled the students of the Royal Veterinary College, a reference to their equine interest. But for Prince Andrew and Sarah Ferguson's wedding, the crowd was undeniably effervescent. There was a saucy, even raunchy atmosphere about the crowd's behaviour that took the cue from the couple's past. Prince Andrew's life as a sailor, his string of previous conquests and rumours of his bride's past love life seemed at odds with a traditional wedding. Predictably, the most common chant of the crowds was the song, 'All the nice girls love a sailor', but, in true music hall fashion, the refrain 'Ship ahoy' was changed to 'Naughty boy!' It was as if the crowd felt they had a perfect licence to treat this occasion as a celebration for one of their own.

However, those hundreds of thousands of people who turned out to line the two processional routes were unabashed monarchists, not even excepting the many foreign tourists. Theirs was not only an active demonstration of loyalty to the Queen and the system of monarchy, but also one of enjoyment of the whole, magnificent spectacle. For generations, loyal subjects have drawn strength from proximity to their sovereign. During the Second World War, crowds gathered at Buckingham Palace, not only to celebrate victory, but in times of defeat as well. Crowds invariably form outside the Palace at the hint of an announcement of a birth, an engagement, a death or even the return of a member of the Royal Family from a lengthy foreign tour. After Prince Charles was born in the Buhl Room on the front of Buckingham Palace, the police had to ask the jubilant crowd for quiet so that the then Princess Elizabeth could sleep: she did not make the same mistake for the birth of Prince Andrew, choosing the quieter Belgian Suite to the rear of the Palace, although the crowds were equally large. Whatever the royal occasion, the motivation of those 'Palace gatherers' for just being there was the same, namely a touching, deep-felt wish to involve themselves with history and the monarchy.

Not everyone, of course, was enamoured of royal weddings. There were those, identified by the *Sun* newspaper as 'sour folk' or 'spoil sports' who 'stroll among closed shops in deserted town centres, or drive along silent roads. At home, some of them keep their curtains open and their tellies switched obstinately off'. Some organised day-trips to republican France, but when the eleven Labour members of the Clay Cross Parish Council in Derbyshire declared it a Republican Day, the residents draped the town in Union flags and extra bunting. One pub, the Travellers, in Rotherham in the 'republic of South Yorkshire' declared itself a 'monarchist free zone', banning its customers from even referring to 'the event in London'.

Despite these 'spoil-sports', the verdict on both weddings was that royalty was 'The Greatest Show on Earth'. Out came the predictable, self-congratulatory line, 'the-sort-of-thing-we-do-so-well'. But both weddings *were* done-so-well: the making of a public spectacle out of a private occasion, the monarchy sharing their family weddings with anybody and everybody who cared to join in. Such public royal weddings, however, are comparatively recent affairs. In the past weddings were held in private, either at Windsor or St James's Palace. The modern style of royal weddings only started after the First World War, when Princess Patricia, daughter of the Duke of Connaught married Captain Alexander Ramsay in 1919. The 'tradition' was continued ever since. (Before that, the crowds had to be content with a glimpse of the newly-married couple on their way to the station at the start of their honeymoon.)

A royal wedding today is a great occasion: it gives great pleasure to millions, financial reward to some, and exhausts all who are even remotely part of it. The polished result belies the hard work that goes into it. Both these royal weddings were the culmination of months of hard work and frayed nerves; the co-ordination of thousands, directly, and indirectly, working towards the same end. However, so perfect was the planning, the orchestration and the execution of the two occasions, that both needed the odd, diverting error to make them human: the horses than panicked and bolted with their frantic troopers (or colonel), the guardsmen who fainted, right up to the fluffed lines in the marriage ceremony of both couples.

One of the great advantages of a commoner marrying into the Royal Family, at least for the parents, is that the wedding is organised, and paid for, by others. (The Queen personally made a large contribution to the cost of both weddings, with the remainder being borne by the State). As neither wedding was a State occasion, their organisation fell on the Queen's Household, as opposed to the Earl Marshall, who is responsible for such State occasions as the Coronation, the Investiture of the Prince of Wales, State funerals, and the like. 'Strictly speaking, the wedding is a private affair although there will be trappings of State', pronounced the Lord Chamberlain, Lord MacLean – an old hand at the game, having masterminded Princess Anne's wedding before that of her elder brother. It was the Earl of Airlie, Princess Alexandra's brother-in-law, the present Lord Chamberlain, who organised Prince Andrew's and Sarah Ferguson's wedding.

The organisation was enormously complicated with so many different factions, internal and external, to co-ordinate, not least the wishes of the two Princes and their *fiancées*.

Prince Andrew and Sarah Ferguson's wedding was virtually a re-run of the Prince and Princess of Wales's wedding, just five years on but on a slightly smaller scale – fewer guests to invite, fewer to seat in the Abbey, fewer wedding presents to deal with, and so on.

The intervening five months for Lady Diana Spencer (only four months for Sarah Ferguson) between engagement and wedding seemed hardly long enough for either of them to prepare for their weddings, let alone their future as members of the Royal Family. Although all the technical details were managed by the Lord Chamberlain's office, it was still, after all, *their* wedding, *their* day. Apart from choosing their favourite hymns (Lady Diana chose 'I vow to thee my country'), the scope for the two girls putting their mark on their wedding day was obviously limited. However, their individuality came to the fore with the wedding dresses they commissioned. Designing the dress for a royal wedding is every couturier's dream, for besides the obvious financial reward, it brings instant, worldwide recognition and fame.

Predictably, the wedding dresses exactly reflected the characters, and moods, of the two royal brides and the mood of their weddings. For Lady Diana Spencer, David and Elizabeth Emanuel, a young husband and wife team, wanted 'to make her look just like a fairy-tale princess' and, to a point, they succeeded. The 'sculptured volume of the ivory silk taffeta crinoline, the massy importance of the broadened shoulders and full sleeves, the richness of the old lace and the hand-embroidered mother-of-pearl and seed pearls, the layers of tulle, the flounces, the taffeta bows and 25 foot train spoke more of grandeur than of romance'[2] wrote one commentator. But 'romance' was only too evidently going to be the key word after the television cameras' first glimpse of the bride through the windows of the glass coach. Shyly smiling through a 'cloudy mass of mother-of-pearl spangled tulle, held in place by the Spencer tiara',[3] the Princess seemed to make the lenses of the cameras mist up. Such was the mood of the day, that there can have been very few who when they first saw the bride, so slender, poised and elegant, were not touched by that romance.

The Carrickmacross lace that made up the panels to the dress had once belonged to Queen Mary, and was therefore 'something old'; the taffeta spun from the life-efforts of British silk-worms was new, the Spencer tiara and her mother's earrings were borrowed while the bow sewn into the hem of the dress was blue. In keeping with a royal tradition, a few hairs from the seamstress's head were sewn into the hem, an idea passed on by Susan Small who designed Princess Anne's wedding dress.

Before her wedding, Sarah Ferguson would not be drawn on her dress but was determined 'that it is going to be quite unlike anything else.' And it was. The wedding dress that Lindka Cierach designed was exactly right for her. It was a clever combination of different historical themes. It had medieval pointed sleeves, Renaissance embroidery on the bodice and a more than passing resemblance to the Queen's own wedding dress of 1948. It reflected the bride's pronounced sense of fun, with the intricate bead-work on the bodice of bees and thistles from her new coat of arms, and the large A for Andrew. Naval anchors and crossed hearts decorated the $17\frac{1}{2}$ foot train. The dress had its own romantic style, one that transformed an undeniably well-rounded figure into one of elegance and regality. But if the Princess of Wales had been a blushing English rose, the Duchess of York was altogether less ethereal.

In the plethora of mush that gushed from the media before her wedding came one particular horror: 'The silkworms that worked for Diana are working for Sarah now!' Although it conjures up a bizarre picture of rows of royal silk-worms munching on mulberry leaves, it is not only biologically inaccurate, it is factually wrong too – the Princess of Wales's silk was English, the Duchess of York's was from Italy. Her shoes were made of English silk-satin and embroidered with bows, ribbons and a bee motif designed by an Italian, Manolo Blahnik.

But despite the richness of the fabrics, the design and the ornamentation, there was still a bucolic quality about her. A country girl at heart, Sarah went to the altar like a May Day bride, a cascade of Titian curls falling from a circlet of lily-of-the-valley, individual cream lily petals and clusters of cream roses and gardenias. That headdress was later replaced by a leaf scroll and diamond collet tiara mounted in platinum, loaned by a friend in the best wedding tradition.

The two brides' choice of designers was almost predictable. Lady Diana Spencer already knew, liked, and suited the Emanuels' work, and their particular Neo-romantic style. Like Princess Anne's wedding dress, it was high fashion of its time. (Susan Small was a complete departure from the more traditional royal couturier houses of Norman Hartnell, who designed Princess Margaret's wedding dress, and Hardy Amies.) The choice of Lindka Cierach by Sarah Ferguson was also typical. Unlike the Emanuels who were not known for their wedding dresses, she specialised in them, her clients being drawn from the richer landed gentry. But the immediate effect of both dresses was arresting; the one against the red carpet of St Paul's Cathedral, the other against the blue of Westminster Abbey.

In his address at Princess Elizabeth and the Duke of Edinburgh's wedding, Dr Geoffrey Fisher, the Archbishop of Canterbury, declared beneath the pomp and pageantry, the essence of the ceremony was 'exactly the same as it would be for any cottager who might be married this afternoon in a small country church in a remote village in the dales.' The same message has been given by subsequent Archbishops at every royal wedding since, although for Lady Diana's wedding it was the Dean of St Paul's who described it as a 'village wedding in the presence of millions through TV.' But with such backcloths as the Cathedral and the Abbey, the waves of clerics in their gorgeous copes, the flowers and the splashes of colour of the Yeoman of the Guard and Gentlemen at Arms, the choirs and the trumpeters, and not least the presence of television cameras, it was hard to think of the occasions in those terms. It was a far cry from Dr Cosmo

Lang, Achbishop of Canterbury, forbidding the wedding service of the Duke and Duchess of York (George VI and Queen Elizabeth) to be broadcast from Westminster Abbey in case 'men in public houses would be listening with their hats on.'

It is every bride's 'right' to feel nervous on her wedding day. For the royal brides, the tension is multiplied one hundredfold. Not only were their weddings in the 'public domain', they were also becoming the latest members of the Royal Family. The ordeal can only have been considerably worse for Lady Diana than for her friend, Sarah Ferguson. She was six years younger at the time of her marriage and so considerably less 'wordly wise'. Hers was a royal wedding; Sarah Ferguson's little more than a very grand society wedding. With the longer aisle of St Paul's, Lady Diana's procession to the altar was daunting: 'I was so nervous', she admitted later, 'that I hardly knew what I was doing.' Where Major Ronald Ferguson marched his daughter up the aisle like a trooper, Lady Diana had to support her ailing father, or, as Adrian Mole, the $13\frac{3}{4}$-year-old diarist, had it, 'Lady Diana melted my heartstrings in her dirty white dress. She even helped an old man up the aisle. I thought it was very kind of her considering it was her wedding day.'[4]

Both ceremonies, however, were stolid, British to the core and traditional. Both used the old order of service from the Book of Common Prayer; both chose strident anthems by Elgar, stirring music by Holst and Mendelssohn (honorary British). The Archbishop of Canterbury married them, Lady Diana mixing up her husband's names and the Prince of Wales forgetting to endow her with all his 'worldly goods', while Sarah Ferguson, who professed to be word perfect, slipped an extra 'Christian' into her spouse's name. Sarah promised to obey, surprisingly Lady Diana did not. Whatever the jumbles with names there could be no doubt what had happened at the two altars. Lady Diana became the Princess of Wales, Sarah the Duchess of York. (The Queen cut it fine in creating Prince Andrew Duke of York, Earl of Inverness and Baron Killyleagh just ninety minutes before the ceremony; a close run thing as no son of a sovereign has not been a Duke when wed for the last six centuries.)

The two ceremonies rumbled to a close. The Speaker, George Thomas, read the lesson in his lilting, Welsh voice for the Prince and Princess of Wales; the Prince of Wales, denied any official function, read the lesson at his brother's wedding. Prayers were said by the clergy of every denomination, and, as the registers were being signed, anthems were sung and children fidgeted. Then, to the blast of trumpets worthy of Jericho came the triumphal processions down the aisle, the brides pausing to sink a deep curtsey to the Queen. One of the most spectacular shots of Lady Diana's wedding was from the roof of the Great Dome of St Paul's. It embraced the whole magnificent scene: the Princess of Wales, her long train flowing behind her on the red carpet, on the arm of her husband, followed by her bridesmaids and pages, his supporters (his two brothers), amidst a rich sea of colour - copes and capes, uniforms and robes, dresses and a full panoply of hats.

Then the return processions to Buckingham Palace: both with escorts from the Household Cavalry. As commoners, both brides were only entitled to mounted police escorts, but as Major Ferguson had commanded the Sovereign's Escort for so many years, his daughter was given an escort of Life Guards (once, in a fit of over-enthusiasm on escort-duty, he rode up alongside the Queen who reproved him with 'they've come to see me, Ronald, not you').

Meanwhile the crowds became restless, chanting for 'Lady Di' and 'S-A-R-A-H'. Their enthusiasm was justly rewarded with the series of balcony appearances. At the first appearance, the Prince of Wales coyly kissed the hand of his bride; at the next, at the suggestion of Prince Andrew and to the intense delight of the crowd and photographers looking for a front cover, they kissed on the lips. Such a thing would have seemed unthinkable even a few years before. Princess Anne and Captain Mark Phillips barely held hands, but once a kiss had been seen once, in true royal fashion it had become a tradition. The crowd called for a kiss of the Duke and Duchess of York on their first balcony appearance.

They obliged, 'not a moth's kiss, but a smacking naval kiss, like a tyre explosion, or as if he were trying to clear the drains'.[5]

'A princely marriage is a brilliant edition of universal fact and as such it rivets mankind,' wrote Walter Bagehot. Although written in the 1870s, the views of that extraordinarily prophetic reviewer of the British monarchy are as true today as they were then. Princess Patricia of Connaught's wedding brought a bright diversion after the First World War: Princess Mary's wedding and the Duke of York's marriage to the present Queen Elizabeth the Queen Mother were both highlights of an otherwise grim time in the early years of the Depression. When Princess Elizabeth married in those bleak days soon after the Second World War, Winston Churchill described it as 'a flash of colour on the hard road we have to travel.' Manny Shinwell, Labour Secretary of State for War, also saw the appeal of such a royal spectacle and made sure that there were enough scarlet uniforms for the Household Cavalry.

Although no panacea for a nation's ills, the royal wedding was seen as more than a diversion to the appalling race riots of Toxteth and Southall, or the hunger strikes of Catholics in Northern Ireland. (Russian television informed its viewers that 'London hopes that the sound of wedding bells will drown out the sound of the shooting in Ireland.') Sarah Ferguson's wedding was also set against a backdrop of national ills. Unemployment was running at a record $3\frac{1}{4}$ million, with 13.7 per cent of the population out of work, the growth of industrial wastelands and, after the Anglo-Irish Agreement, the Protestant terrorists of Northern Ireland up in arms. Coincidentally, the Prime Minister, Margaret Thatcher, was low in popularity according to the opinion polls at the time of both weddings. The first was prior to the Falklands conflict, the second a year before her election for her third term.

A royal occasion is however more than a diversion from political turmoil and industrial strife. It is a way in which the British can demonstrate national unity without having to declare war. Most of the successful and lasting monarchies today are of Protestant countries. There, the people look to the monarchy for that same ritual and 'theatre' that the church provides in Catholic countries. The Marxists, on the other hand, would have it that such a display is merely a 'religious con-job designed to distract the populace from their true interests as members of the working class.' To them, such occasions must show Britain up as a class-ridden society: the privileged on the inside making a spectacle for the mob – the circuses provided by the Roman emperors to amuse the rabble. However, without the privileged making the spectacle, there would be nothing for the underprivileged to enjoy. As Peregrine Worsthorne wrote:

> Just as a pyramid can not exist without its pinnacle and a broad base, neither can a royal occasion like a Royal Wedding ... There is so much more to an historic nation than class divisions, shared emotions, memories, sentiments, not to mention language and culture and above all, of course, love of country. But only the monarchy nowadays seems capable of doing justice to this sense of nationhood, which is why these royal occasions are beginning to take on a far more than a symbolic significance.[6]

Above all, both royal weddings were a media dream: real life stories that could run and run, without fear of going stale. Whenever there was not much news there was always something royal for the front page: a marriage in jeopardy, a baby on the way – always an 'exclusive' inside story revealing nothing at all. *The Socialist Worker* saw the royal wedding as 'Big Ears marries Noddy, a fairy tale come true'. The *Washington Post* could only expire in an orgasm of: 'Lovely, lovely, lovely. Lovely, lovely, lovely'. Gushing Clive Barnes in the *New York Post* thought 'Fergie looked – and behaved – as if she were making a commercial for radiance.' The Argentine newspaper, *Cronica*, with the Falklands War a bitter memory, described Prince Andrew's wedding as a 'luxurious and entertaining event at the court of the pirates.' But it was the television coverage of the two weddings that was most staggering.

The BBC and Independent television covered every inch of the route, every moment of the day. They in turn gave or sold their pictures, live, to the television companies around the world. The Prince and Princess of Wales's wedding was the biggest-ever television broadcast with over 700 million viewers. Only 500 million viewers watched the Duke and Duchess of York's. Real and self-styled 'royal experts' were at a premium, summoned to pontificate on every television channel around the world. The three network companies, CBS, NBC and ABC from the United States all sent over the top anchors (presenters) of their early evening news programmes to cover Prince Charles's wedding. For the Yorks, they fielded their 'B team' from the morning news.

This massive media coverage of both weddings was a baptism by fire. From their wedding days the Princess of Wales and the Duchess of York had to live with another eye. The camera lens thenceforward would accompany them wherever they went in public and often when they would believe themselves to be private. Through the camera the Princess of Wales, and to a lesser extent the Duchess of York, have become the most famous women in the world. But what is remarkable is that extraordinary fame, and the effect it has on themselves, the public and the monarchy.

To the Palace Born

'If he did not exist, then he would have to have been invented' said the pundits of Prince Philip when he married the then Princess Elizabeth. The same, however, could almost be said of Lady Diana Spencer on her engagement to their eldest son. From an early age, the Prince of Wales realised he was 'different from what other men are', particularly with his choice of bride. In his first television interview just before his Investiture, he touchingly admitted that:

> It's awfully difficult, because you've got to remember that when you marry, in my position, you've got to marry someone who, perhaps, is going to be Queen. You've got to choose someone very carefully, I think, who could fulfil this particular role, and it has got to be somebody pretty unusual ... The one advantage about marrying a princess, for instance, or somebody from a royal family, is that they do know what happens.[1]

Apart from knowing the 'form', marrying a princess of royal blood at least ensured suitability: so 'suitable' was Princess May of Teck that when her fiancé, the Duke of Clarence, Heir Presumptive died, she was immediately affianced to the next in line, his younger brother, the Duke of York, the future George V. It was not such an old-fashioned idea either; it was said that the Queen, with her unsurpassed knowledge on every thoroughbred bloodline and the relative value of their breeding potential, was in favour of blood royal marrying royal blood (as she herself had so successfully done), at least for the Heir Apparent. But by the time the Prince had turned thirty, 'the right age for marriage' as he once inadvertently said, there were no suitable royal princesses for him even to contemplate marrying: in fact, the only two were Princess Caroline of Monaco and Princess Marie-Astrid of Luxembourg, and they were out of the running as both were Catholics.

Where at the turn of the century it would have been unthinkable for the Heir Apparent to marry a commoner for love, by the 1980s the Prince of Wales could have married anyone in the world, saving of course a Catholic or a divorcee. But this huge choice made the 'task' of finding a wife for himself more difficult, rather than easier. The problem, as he was only too aware, was to find someone acceptable by today's standards. As he said, 'To me, marriage – which may be for fifty years – seems to me to be one of the biggest and most responsible steps to be taken in one's life.'[2]

For Prince Charles, there was little question of opting out. Of course, divorcees have long been received at Court – it would be a very empty place if they were barred: the ban would start with Princess Margaret and her cousin, Prince Michael of Kent who is married to a divorced woman. But as Prince Charles said, 'the last thing I could possibly entertain is getting divorced.... My marriage has to be forever'.[3] In fact, constitutionally he was not quite correct. There are precedents. Henry VIII started the rot by divorcing twice, and George I was divorced before he came to the throne. There is nothing to stop the Sovereign divorcing, only remarrying afterwards. However, divorce of the heir apparent, the next Defender of the Faith, is legal but not palatable to the people. Either way, such a step was unthinkable to a man on the brink of marriage.

The basic criteria of the royal wife are straight forward enough:

besides such attributes as beauty, charm, and a degree of intelligence, not hard to find in the modern girl, she has to be prepared to become royal with all that that entails, both good and bad, exciting and tedious. The future queen has to be fertile, from a respectable background, and, above all, beyond reproach. She should be untarnished, without what is euphemistically called a 'past'. True to the fairy tale tradition, as indeed in royal lore and public acceptability, the future Queen of England has to be a virgin bride. That she should be in love with her prince as well will surely come as a bonus. That Prince Charles should find someone who fitted such a description on all counts, in the 1980s, defied belief.

Although he greatly enjoyed his bachelor life, the Prince of Wales equally wanted to get married. As the pressure, and necessity, for him to marry and have children increased as the years passed, it became more and more difficult for him to find that ideal wife. His seeming reluctance to marry, or indeed to consort with anyone remotely 'suitable', was a constant source of friction between him and his father. His 'You better get on with it Charles, or there won't be anyone left' was more than just a tease. Even the press, usually so keen to name his future bride, were losing heart. Once, in desperation, the *Daily Express* even announced: 'Charles to marry [Princess] Astrid. Official.'[4] A definite mistake, as the Press Office at Buckingham Palace was quick to point out:

> They are not getting engaged this Monday, next Monday, the Monday after or any other Monday, Tuesday, Wednesday or Thursday. They do not know each other, and people who do not know each other do not get engaged. The Royal Family does not go in for arranged marriages.

As the denial purported to have come from the Prince himself, the over-reaction to a stupid headline had the ring of coming from a man who was not only heartily sick of false rumours (he should have been used to them having suffered from them virtually since the day he was born), but also of a desperate man. Drawing parallel's between him and his great-uncle, the Duke of

Windsor, who remained a bachelor until his forties only to end up in the clutches of a twice-divorced American, became closer as the years rolled by. Then, quite suddenly, as if by some magical, Royal, computer dating system, he found her.

The mythical Lord High Chamberlain (The Kindest and Best of Men) in Hilaire Belloc's *Godolphin Horn* took:

> A Perfectly Enormous Book
> Called *People Qualified to Be
> Attendant on His Majesty*

If some such similar book (with all too few entries today) had been consulted for those 'qualified to be' the wife of the Prince of Wales, Lady Diana Spencer would surely have headed the list. Even though she was so eminently suitable in every way to be his future queen, it was indeed miraculous that he recognised it in time, or, as is equally likely, had it pointed out to him. In retrospect, he must have realised that she represented his last chance to find such a wife. It was equally remarkable that he could recognise in that rather shy, somewhat gauche girl of nineteen, albeit with an endearing, sideways glance, the striking, self confident woman she became so soon after her engagement.

On the face of it, Lady Diana Spencer was not the kind of girl instantly to attract the Prince of Wales. Besides a love of the country, they had little immediately in common. Nor was she of the ranks of his *anciennes amours*, who, besides being beautiful, were uniformly intelligent, quick-witted and sophisticated. There was always something definite that he could respond to in them, from a shared love of horses, particularly hunting and team chasing (like a hunt race) to philanthropy – an early girlfriend, Davina Sheffield, had worked in a Vietnamese orphanage before the fall of Saigon. Others, like Anna Wallace, were headstrong. That, in fact, was her undoing. His girlfriend for nine months, she attended the ball at Windsor Castle to mark Queen Elizabeth the Queen Mother's eightieth birthday only to be neglected by him for the whole evening. She stormed out in a fury, reportedly telling him: 'Don't ever ignore me like that again! And nobody –

not even you – behaves that way to me.' Her departure left him bruised and vulnerable. Lady Diana, who followed soon after the fiery Miss Wallace's departure, was, despite her slender years, clearly out of a different mould. But her attributes, not all of her own making, lay in other quarters. But it was those very differences from these worldly-wise women that was to appeal to him in the end. Equally important, she had a massive, world-wide appeal, not just as the future wife of the Prince of Wales, but in her own right.

For a start, Lady Diana was English, although the genealogists would carve her up as having English, Scottish, Irish, and Welsh blood, not to mention a dash of American and Polish – all of which was thoroughly acceptable in the future Queen of England. The injection of some true British blood would assure anew the long overdue Anglicisation of the Royal Family (it was the Scottish Queen Elizabeth the Queen Mother who finally thinned that long line of near pure German and Danish blood). Like the Queen Mother, the Princess of Wales comes from one of the most aristocratic families in the country, a surprisingly endearing factor in itself in a world where not everyone 'loves a lord'. The tabloids always referred to her, indeed some still do, as Lady Di, or as the French would have it 'La-DiDi'. At least they got her title right. She is descended, albeit illegitimately, several times from the Stuart Kings of England, something the Prince of Wales can not claim. In fact, her claim to true royal blood could have been absolute had an earlier Lady Diana Spencer not turned down Frederick Louis, Prince of Wales, son of George II (he also missed out on a much needed £100,000 dowry).

Lady Diana's instant popularity with the public is intriguing. There was no 'Hollywood' glamour about her: she was not a sizzling starlet on her way to stardom. Her parents were not even famous. What she was, was a 'thoroughly nice girl' who bites her finger nails; the typical girl next door that mothers hope their sons will end up marrying. She lived a simple, uncomplicated life working not 'awfully' hard as a helper in a kindergarten, sharing a flat (hers) with three other 'awfully' nice girls, having a jolly

Diana Spencer, aged nearly three, at the
wedding of her uncle, Lord Fermoy.

Sarah Ferguson, aged three.

Sarah Ferguson in the Glass Coach on her way to Westminster Abbey, 24 July 1986.

Two old friends, Lady Diana Spencer and Sarah Ferguson, at Cowdray Park polo ground, June 1980.

The wedding of the century: The Prince and Princess of Wales returning from St Paul's Cathedral,
29 July 1981

The photographer, Albert Watson, used a hooter to attract everyone's attention
for the jolly, family wedding photograph of the Duke and Duchess of York.

A large teddy bear accompanied the Duke and Duchess of York on the first leg of their honeymoon.

The Princess of Wales, clearly in her element with children, at a Dr Barnardo's day centre at Brixton.

The Prince of Wales much in the background as the Princess claims the attention at a joint visit to Brixton.

The Duchess of York spreading cheer at a centre for handicapped children in Southampton.

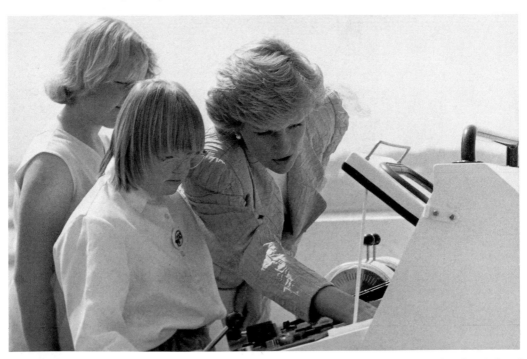

The Princess of Wales has all the patience and understanding when with handicapped and underprivileged children, as here on the bridge of the *Queen Elizabeth II*.

Three sisters-in-law at the Cenotaph, Whitehall, on Remembrance Sunday, 1987.

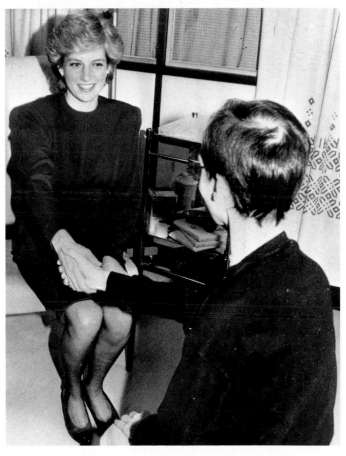

The photograph that showed there was nothing to fear from
shaking hands with a terminal Aids victim.

A family reception, standing exactly in order of precedence, for the King of Morocco.

The Duke and Duchess of York on an official visit to York in 1987.

time giving dinner parties and going to the cinema, and leaving London for the weekend on Fridays. Her clothes were typically 'Sloane'; like her, safe and sensible. She was not intellectual or sophisticated. A natural for the women's and society magazine market, but certainly not the sort of girl to appeal to the readership of the world's more sensationalist press. But captivate them all, she did.

She was eminently acceptable to the Royal Family too. As her father, Earl Spencer, was to point out: 'My family have served the Royal Family for generations', not least the Queen Mother who has, or has had, both of Lady Diana's grandmothers and four of her great-aunts as ladies-in-waiting, Woman of the Bedchamber or Mistress of the Robes. As *The Times* put it, on the wedding day, the Queen Mother 'will have as many Spencers around her as the bride'. Also, the Royal Family have stood sponsor (royal parlance for godparent) for members of the Spencer family since the time of George III. However, at Court for 'service' read friendship.

The links of service and friendship between Lady Diana's family and the Royal Family could not have been closer. They were further strengthened when that 'true Norfolk squire', George V, leased Park House, a large and incommodious pile on his Sandringham Estate to her maternal grandparents, Lord and Lady Fermoy. After the king died, George VI and Queen Elizabeth became their firm friends, both men sharing a passion for shooting. Lady Diana's mother, the Hon Frances Roche, was born there, a mere twelve years before her son-in-law. She, in turn, was married from there, a young bride of eighteen, to Viscount Althorp (the present Earl Spencer), Equerry to George VI, and then to the present Queen on the death of her father. Most significantly of all, the Althorps took over Park House in 1955 when Lord Fermoy died and his widow went to live in London.

The Honourable Diana Spencer (as she was before her father succeeded to the Earldom), was born and brought up for the first thirteen years of her life at Park House. In those early years, the Royal Family spent the whole of Christmas and well into the New

Year at Sandringham. Later, when the family expanded with a royal baby-boom, the House was found to be too 'snug a fit' for them all, so they repaired to Windsor Castle for Christmas and the honoured few were invited to Sandringham for the New Year and the shoots that followed. After that, Sandringham only figured slightly in the annual royal migration: occasionally they would open up the house for a weekend, more often, they would stay at Wood Farm, a comfortable farmhouse on the estate.

Thus the picture that certain of the tabloid press tried to create of the little girl running across the lawns that separated the two houses, walking into the drawing room and calling the Queen 'Aunt Lillibet' is totally spurious. That said, when the Royal Family was in residence, the Spencer children would, like all their neighbours and friends, be included at some stage in their festivities, a children's party, later a children's dance, or the annual estate party. Equally, the younger members of the Royal Family would be invited back to Park House for their parties or meet the Spencer children at their neighbours' houses. A contemporary of the younger royals, 'she used to gang up with Prince Andrew'. Having grown up in the shadow of a royal home, the young Diana Spencer would be quite used to meeting the Queen and the rest of the Royal Family, both in their house and her own home. None of them would hold any terror for her if, say, they met out on a walk on the estate, any more than any other of their grander Norfolk neighbours. (The Royal Family have a habit of 'dropping in', as many an unprepared neighbour will testify.) Thus, she instinctively knew how to behave with them, and what was expected of her in return.

Her contact with the Royal Family was further boosted, although somewhat tangentially, when her sister, Sarah, who had known Prince Charles for most of her life, accompanied him for a few months to various social functions. The press escalated their easy, uncomplicated friendship into marital proportions and eventually Sarah was forced into making her position known: 'I'm not in love with him ... and I wouldn't marry anyone I didn't love, whether it was the dustman or the King of England.

If he asked me, I would turn him down.' That said, the press who had dogged her every move, dropped her and subsequently she did exactly what she said she would do and married (a farmer, Neil McCorquodale), for love and love alone. Another strong point of contact with the Royal Family came when her sister, Jane, married Robert Fellowes, a Norfolk neighbour who is assistant Private Secretary to the Queen. Thus, when the Prince of Wales pointed out the advantages of marrying a princess as they 'know what happens', Lady Diana, although not a princess, came closer than most through her childhood contacts and those long lines of courtiers, past and present, within her family.

But most strongly in Lady Diana Spencer's favour was 'her total lack of a past'. Many of the Prince of Wales's girlfriends, often to his deep disappointment, fell by the wayside when a past affair was discovered by the press. One case in point was Davina Sheffield whose former lover revealed that, unofficially engaged, they had lived together in a cottage near Winchester. Today, for anyone else, such a story would hardly raise an eyebrow, let alone full-scale coverage in the press, but for a possible future wife of the Prince of Wales, it made front page news. Try as they might, exhaustive research by the tabloids revealed nothing in Lady Diana's past. The romantic novelist, Barbara Cartland, mother of the second Countess Spencer, declared her as 'purity itself', even 'a perfect Barbara Cartland heroine', while her uncle, Lord Fermoy, felt it incumbent on himself to declare to an astonished press corps that 'Lady Diana, I can assure you, has never had a lover. There is no such thing as her ever having a past'. Suddenly, 'purity' became fashionable (as did practically everything connected with Lady Diana after her engagement). Tina Brown, the then editor of *Tatler*, writing of her 'unexpected bonus of extreme youth' declared that she:

> comes from a born-again generation of old fashioned girls who choose to play it safe rather than have safety chosen for them. The career girls, the rebels, the bolters, the experimenters are now among the older generation. They are, in fact, among the age group of her sisters' friends, whom Lady Diana was able

to observe at length and, in doing so, draw her own conclusions about the merits or otherwise of more adventurous values. As she cuts the tape, kisses the baby or waves from the royal balcony she has one unique royal advantage. She knows what she's missed and she doesn't care.

Leaving nothing to chance, Lady Diana was reputedly given a gynaecological test to make sure she could bear children ('I like to give myself heirs', the Prince once punned in a Cambridge review). It would be invidious to imagine what would have happened had the tests proved negative.

Even ten years before, what could have been a flaw to this perfect match was the fact that Lady Diana's parents were divorced. At that time, 1969, divorce was still not wholly acceptable at Court (it was only 14 years since divorced couples were barred from the Royal Enclosure at the Royal Meeting at Ascot). For a long time, even the Queen's first cousin, the Earl of Harewood (his mother was the Princess Royal, sister of George VI) was not received at Court as he was divorced and had remarried. However, he and his divorced brother, the Honourable Gerald Lascelles, both went to the two Royal Weddings: it would have been somewhat hypocritical not to ask them with both the bride's parents being divorced, and, in the case of the Princess of Wales, remarried to divorcees.

As with many an aristocratic divorce, the Althorps' turned out to be a messy affair attracting the maximum publicity. It was fought bloodily in court, with action for cruelty and counter-action for adultery. The intimate details were blazoned over the tabloid press, they were buzzed around the dinner tables of the grander Norfolk houses. It has been suggested that that unwanted attention of the press affected the eight-year-old Diana, giving her the experience to cope with her own pre-engagement hassle with the world's press. It is extremely unlikely that the girl even saw a newspaper, let alone a reporter at the time. Her nanny shielded her from outside pressures, as did her sisters, Sarah and Jane. Being that much older, they would have known exactly what was going on (if they did not, their schoolfriends certainly would have told them). The divorce case itself can have made very little difference to her life as her parents had separated two years before, her mother living in her flat in Cadogan Place, London, her father remaining at Park House and farming not far away. But the bitterness of their parents' separation, and subsequent divorce, deeply affected them all, and there were times when their lives were difficult and strained.

What is significant, however, is the part played in the separation, divorce, and the subsequent bringing up of the children by Ruth, Lady Fermoy, their maternal grandmother. Lord Althorp was granted custody of the children, although their mother, of course, shared them in the school holidays (before the divorce, Diana and her brother, Charles, lived with their mother and went to school in London). Holidays were spent either with her mother and stepfather, Peter Shand Kydd and his family at Chichester, West Sussex, or at Park House. Unlike his wife, Lord Althorp did not marry again, at least not until several years later. To bridge the gap left by Lady Althorp, her mother stepped in to care for the children during those holidays at home. She was one of Queen Elizabeth the Queen Mother's closest friends, and that friendship naturally brought Diana into closer contact with the Queen Mother. Later, there were the inevitable comparisons between these two Earls' daughters who married into the Royal Family. The Queen Mother who has known Diana 'since she was so high', has admitted that she took these comparisons 'as a high compliment'. Likewise, the Queen Mother makes no secret of her affection for her first grandchild, the Prince of Wales (he, too, admits to being 'hopelessly biased and completely partisan' about her). It would be wrong to suggest that these two old friends, Lady Fermoy and the Queen Mother, manipulated their grandchildren into marrying one with another, but they certainly smoothed the tricky path, provided 'safe houses' during the courtship, and most important of all, gave wise counsel to both throughout, as indeed they do today. It was not difficult, however, to accuse Lord Mountbatten of 'manipulating' his family: having succeeded in engineering the then Princess Elizabeth's marriage to his nephew, Prince Philip, he tried again to match-make his granddaughter, Amanda Knatchbull, and his great-nephew, with no result other than they are still firm friends. Safe to say that Lord Mountbatten, 'who rarely took up any book unless it were one of genealogy',[5] would have heartily approved of his great-nephew's choice of Lady Diana Spencer, not only of her breeding, but of her as a person.

Another barrier that Lady Diana Spencer crossed with seeming ease was that she was fully prepared to enter the Royal Family. Put like that, it sounds as if she were taking the veil which, in a sense, she was. Her life was to be no longer her own. As the Queen Mother put it when faced with the same dilemma nearly sixty years before, 'as royalty, [I will] never, never again be free to think or speak or act as I feel I ought to think or speak or act'. In fact, mindful of that daunting prospect, Lady Elizabeth Bowes-Lyon turned down Prince Albert when he first proposed, accepting on the second time of asking. That same, daunting prospect set the fate of earlier romances of the Prince of Wales, not least his romance with the highly intelligent Lade Jane Wellesley, daughter of the Duke of Wellington.

On the day of the Prince of Wales's and Lady Diana's engagement, there were two telling remarks made by each of them in their television interview. When asked if she found it (her answer to his proposal) a hard decision, she replied without a moment's hesitation:

> I had a long time to think about it ... but it wasn't a difficult decision in the end. It's what I wanted – it's what I want.

This is not the reply of a shy, self-effacing, young girl but of one who knows her own mind. Although the inner workings of constitutional history were far beyond her, she knew enough of what her future held as the Princess of Wales and to 'take' Prince Charles on, not just as a husband, but as a member of the Royal Family; her fiancé called it bravery. To the question, 'And I suppose in love?', she blushed and instantly replied 'Of course!' with the confidence of a mature woman.

The Prince of Wales had proposed to her in his rooms at Buckingham Palace 'two or three days before she went to Australia,' offering her that time to think about it. Her reply was an instant 'Yes', although she did agree to consider the proposal and discuss it all with her mother in Australia in the intervening three weeks. It would appear by her prompt reply (her own words) to his proposal, and indeed all her other answers, that she had made her mind up long before that she would accept him if he asked. In an interview with Madame Yersin, the headmistress of her finishing school in Switzerland, it was revealed that 'She [Lady Diana] was secretly in love with Prince Charles'. Thus, it would appear that her mind was made up from the age of sixteen onwards. It must have been difficult for her at that time when her sister went on a skiing holiday in Switzerland with the Prince of Wales and being forced to wait silently for the outcome. Undoubtedly, early on in their relationship, Sarah confided to her younger sister that, as far as she was concerned, there was no possibility of marriage, but for Lady Diana, as in the oldest and best fairy tales, things had to be bad before they became right.

The Prince of Wales's replies to the interviewers were equally telling. When he too was asked if he was in love, he answered 'Whatever "in love" means'. On the day of the announcement of your engagement, surely you know what 'in love' means? But he had admitted that he did know what it meant in many an interview in the past: 'I have fallen in love with all sorts of girls and fully intend to go on doing so.' Taken at face value, his glib answer, surely regretted afterwards, might have portrayed the truth at that time. There he was, engaged to the most eminently suitable girl in Britain. By saying that he did not know what being 'in love' means, he possibly was not in love *at that time*. If that were so, then the engagement had the ring of the arranged marriage he had been at such pains to dismiss over the Princess Marie-Astrid announcement not seven months before. However, it was all a question of time and of timing.

In their interview before the wedding, she declared that they had first met in 1976 in 'a ploughed field' at Althorp where he thought her 'a jolly and amusing and attractive sixteen-year-old': she found him 'pretty amazing'. Over the next three years after that initial meeting, they met only spasmodically. Still very much as a 'chum' of Prince Andrew's, the Queen asked her to Balmoral in August 1978 as part of the younger set, known as 'Queeny-boppers' of her house party. The Prince of Wales was there at that time and though obviously aware of her, concentrated on his own friends. Although Sarah's public revelation that she would never marry the Prince of Wales naturally put paid to any hint of romance, it did not affect their friendship. The two sisters were invited to Sandringham by the Queen in January of the next year to stay for one of the many shooting parties and again, the Prince was there (at that time, he had been linked with Anna Wallace for four months). Later that summer, Lady Diana was included in various events connected with the Royal Family. She was asked to Cowdray Park, the polo ground in Sussex, in July to watch the finals of the Gold Cup, where the Prince of Wales was playing for *Les Diables Bleus*. There was a ball after at Goodwood House.

Then came the invitation from the Duke of Edinburgh to join his party aboard HMY *Britannia* in early August for Cowes Week. Again, the Prince of Wales was in this party. It was here that she gave a brave demonstration of her renowned 'sense of fun' when she tipped him over on his wind-surfer as he sailed close to the royal yacht. Later that month, Lady Diana was back in Scotland, ostensibly to help her sister Jane with her new baby, but also at the behest of the Queen, for her house party at Balmoral. Then, as the world knows, she was spied watching the Prince of Wales fishing on the River Dee by James Whitaker of the *Daily Star*, and, when her identity was known, her life was never to be the same again. As the Queen Mother said on the day of her engagement, 'When the cat is out of the bag, it is very difficult to stuff it back in again.' However, in this case, there was no cat, and no bag, at least for another five months.

Those intervening years between the meeting in the ploughed field and when the *Daily Star* photograph appeared announcing the new girl in the Prince of Wales's life can hardly be described as a serious courtship, yet virtually within minutes, the tabloid press had them engaged: the right girl, the right result, but somewhat premature. That she was totally in love with him there is no doubt; the Prince of Wales admitted as much in their engagement interview. When asked about the timing of their courtship he replied, 'towards the end of the summer and autumn last year [1980], I began to realise what was going on in my mind, and hers in particular'. Her love had grown from the simple, infatuation of the Prince of Wales, like some schoolgirl's crush on a pop idol or film star, to the real love of the real man. However, the Prince of Wales, a self-confessed romantic, had clearly not fallen for her then in the same way as he had with his other girlfriends in the past.

Convinced that they had discovered the future Princess of Wales, the press would not let go. They escalated the relationship, still very much in its infancy, into marital proportions, with no thought to the true facts, nor indeed to the protagonists themselves. Both the press, and through them the public, instantly warmed to her. But hounding her mercilessly for those five months before her engagement, an action they naturally excused as satisfying public demand, meant that when they did meet, it put their meeting on another footing. The endless speculation as to the exact nature of their relationship, real and supposed (almost exclusively the latter), did have the effect of quickening the pace of their initial courtship and of his eventual proposal.

In retrospect, it may appear that courtship was too strong a word to describe their relationship at that time. They had become great friends. He certainly enjoyed her company, and was amused by her. He could also recognise that, beneath that somewhat shy exterior, was a strength of character, something that could perhaps be moulded, an Eliza Doolittle to his Professor Higgins. They had spent the odd weekend together, platonically, both with the Queen Mother at Birkhall, in Scotland, and with his friends, like Lt Colonel Andrew Parker-Bowles and his wife Camilla (a confidante), in Wiltshire. She had seen him race-ride at Ludlow (backing him each way); he sat between her and Lady Jane Wellesley at the dinner party before the dance given for Princess Margaret to mark her fiftieth birthday. Ten days later, his birthday, the press fervently hoped for the announcement of his engagement (one editor, Sir Larry Lamb of *The Sun* went so far as to bet Nigel Dempster, the *Daily Mail* gossip columnist, £4,000 that it would happen: he lost, of course). Instead, she was spirited into Sandringham that afternoon in an old Ford Cortina. From then on, duty called the Prince of Wales to India, until mid-December, and his family beckoned him to Windsor for Christmas on his return, and Sandringham for the New Year. Lady Diana spent Christmas with her father at Althorp, and saw the New Year in with a flatmate in London before joining the Royal party at Sandringham the day after. There were just three recorded meetings after, another visit to Sandringham, a lunch at High-grove and a dawn foray to the Prince's trainer, Nick Gaselee, at Lambourn, before he went off skiing with his friends, the Palmer-Tomkinsons, to Switzerland. On his return, he invited her to dinner (3 February) and, in his rooms in Buckingham Palace, he asked her to marry him. She accepted there and then, and their engagement was announced three weeks later on her return from Australia. At last there was now a cat, and a bag.

The engagement ended months of speculation, but only height-ened, if possible, the interest in Lady Diana. With the announce-ment came a certain amount of protection for her: she moved, briefly, into Clarence House and then was given a suite of rooms at Buckingham Palace. In fact, she stayed most of the time with her sister Jane beside Kensington Palace and with her mother in Warwick Square, Pimlico. At last, the affianced couple could be together without the attendant 'wild surmise' of the media. It was the time when, in nice old-fashioned parlance, their courtship could begin. The Prince of Wales had always said of his future wife that 'Essentially you must be good friends, and love, I am sure, will grow out of that friendship.' Five months later, on the day of his wedding, there was no doubt that that old romantic was truly in love with his bride and by then, knew full well what 'in love' meant.

The road to the altar and marital bliss for the Duke and Duchess of York could hardly have been more different from that of his elder brother and sister-in-law, the Prince and Princess of Wales. Quite apart from the difference in their ages when they actually married, they are all wildly different characters as well – Prince Andrew, 'at twenty-six [is] some ten years younger than, five times better looking, and half as intelligent as [Prince] Charles'.[6] The sisters-in-law, though great friends, are total opposites too.

Unlike his brother, constitutionally Prince Andrew could have married anyone, at least anyone who would have him. The old taboos of those unacceptable Catholics and divorcees equally applied to him if he wanted to remain in the Royal pecking order, (Prince Michael of Kent had bowed out of the seventeenth place, but then he married not only a divorcee, but a Catholic as well). However, with the births of Princes William and Harry, (what the Duchess of Marlborough described as 'an heir and a spare' when describing her two sons), he was relegated to fourth in line. Just as the Princess of Wales appeared at precisely the right moment (after the departure of Anna Wallace), so Sarah Ferguson's timing coincided with a distinct change in the Prince's life.

Prince Andrew is the eldest of the Queen's 'second' family. His elder brother and sister, the Princess Royal, had grown up and fled the nest while he was still at school – he was just thirteen when his sister married and Prince Charles was serving in the Royal Navy. It was when he was packed off to school in Canada at the age of seventeen, his first outing away from the strictures of home and school, that this handsome young prince began to turn the heads of the first of a very long line of pretty (often indiscreet) girls and, equally, to have his head turned by them, frequently with disastrous results. His apt, rhyming sobriquet 'Randy Andy', coined by his classmates, was to stick to the day of his wedding. On leaving school and joining the Royal Navy, his antics became a natural for the tabloid press.

He was, and is, a confirmed practical joker. But much more newsworthy was his choice of girlfriends. They were invariably beautiful models, actresses and beauty queens (what the Edwardians termed as chorus girls), hardly the sort of girl for the young royal to marry, but just the kind of girl the young 'Randy Andy' enjoyed being with. Of all his many paramours, he was most smitten with the American-born, soft-porn actress, Koo Stark. It was she who 'guided him from knee-socks to knee-tremblers',[7] and was the girl he took to the Island of Mustique in the West Indies on his return from the Falklands War. The affair was not to last, but his reputation did. Headstrong, he courted disaster: the world's press found him in Mustique, he courted a succession of 'kiss-and-tell' girls who found a ready market for their stories. He was dogged by bad-luck too: a former Buckingham Palace storeman sold his account of 'Queen Koo's romps at the Palace' to the *Sun*. (The Queen herself in an unprecedented move took out a High Court Action to prevent further publication.) Other girlfriends followed, each as beautiful, usually as unsuitable, as the last. It was as if he had to live up to his nickname, a macho-man by day, a member of the demi-monde by night.

Such reports, some apochryphal but mostly with more than a grain of truth, were an obvious cause for concern to his parents. But such behaviour could be excused; after all he was a serving Naval officer and doing what any of his contemporaries was doing, or would like to have been doing had they the chance. What was the last straw, however, happened in California on a visit to raise funds for the British Olympic Federation. Visiting a housing rehabilitation centre, he was invited to spray a wall with white paint: instead, he 'accidentally' turned it on the attendant press corps (in fact only a few flecks of paint actually landed, but the amount was not in question, only the action). The Queen was not amused: his father doubtless expressed his disapproval more strongly. On his return, he was kept very much in check, joining his parents aboard the Royal Yacht as it cruised about the Western Isles off Scotland in the autumn. Somewhat chastened, he led a similar life but kept a lower profile.

The image of the Lothario, joker Prince, however, was merely a façade, one that was dropped in private with true friends and family. He had taken up photography as a serious hobby, converting a bathroom at Buckingham Palace into a dark room. He exhibited his work, published a book of his photographs, *Photographs of Prince Andrew*, and even shot the 1985 Ilford calendar. The photographs were portentous, most being of dark passages, ruined castles set against bleak landscapes and chill skies: the women were distant, unreal or unreachable. When asked by David Frost in an interview if there was a theme to his photography, he made the telling reply, 'Dare I say it? The theme, in fact, is loneliness.' Here was much more the real Prince Andrew. Behind that exterior of flashing teeth in a permanent grin, the brave Falkland's hero with more than a dash of libido and Mountbatten arrogance, a Prince Hooray Henry in other words, was a jolly decent chap, a little lost perhaps, but one desperately trying to express himself.

Were his serious critics asked if he showed any signs of settling down at the age of twenty-six, they would have doubtless replied that he was enjoying his bachelor life too much to even contemplate such a step. But then they did not know the real Prince, nor did they appreciate the prowess of the Princess of Wales to play Cupid. In a BBC interview, Prince Andrew was asked what he would look for in a future bride.

> You know, the honest answer is, I don't know what I am looking for, because I have not had any chance to think about it. It all depends what comes up in the next few years. [But if he did find somebody] it is going to come like a lightning bolt, and you're going to know it there and then.

That lightning bolt was, of course, Sarah Ferguson. As the interview was in October 1985, just four months before he proposed to, and was accepted by her, he was either playing his cards very close to his chest, or the bolt had struck him but he had not yet realised that it had landed. For a start, she was a girl whom he had known all his life. Her father, Major Ronald Ferguson, is a polo chum of the Duke of Edinburgh, and, as with every child of dedicated polo parents they both spent a large part of the summer beside the polo ground. They renewed their childhood friendship in 1983 when staying with the Duke and Duchess of Roxburgh at Floors Castle in the Scottish Border Country.

It was, however, the Princess of Wales who suggested, and the Queen only too readily agreed, that Sarah Ferguson be invited to Windsor Castle for the Royal Meeting at Ascot in June 1985. In their television interview before the marriage, they admitted that 'it' all started at that lunch when he pressed her to eat a chocolate-covered, cream-filled profiterole. She was on a diet. When he refused them himself, she playfully clapped him on the back. Not exactly a lightning bolt, but at least it was a start. 'There are always humble beginnings,' he said, 'it's got to start somewhere.' A little over a year later, they were married, with a little help from their friend.

Just as the two grandmothers eased the path for the Prince and Princess of Wales to be together, so the Princess just 'happened' to be around to smooth the passage of her brother-in-law and Sarah Ferguson. She would invite them both to dinner parties at Kensington Palace, or for the weekend at Highgrove, her home in Gloucestershire. When she visited HMS *Brazen*, Prince Andrew's ship, her friend went along too: she went skiing with the Prince and Princess, without Prince Andrew, at Klosters in Switzerland. Prince Andrew did not need the assistance of his sister-in-law, however, when he proposed to her at Floors Castle, while staying with the Duke and Duchess of Roxburgh. He proposed to her on both knees, she accepted him saying, 'Yes, and if you wake up the next morning, you can tell me it's all a huge joke!' Cupid had succeeded.

It would be churlish to suggest that the Princess of Wales had an ulterior motive in fostering this romance between her brother-in-law and one of her best friends, but were it to come to anything, the advantages to her would be considerable. When they married a little over a year later, the advantages were manifest.

The Princess of Wales is an exact contemporary of Prince

Andrew. They had known each other since the cradle and were great friends. They are fond of each other in a strictly fraternal/sororial way, and she could certainly see beneath that veneer of bravado. She obviously wanted to see him happily married, or if not actually married, at least happy. She was also fond of Sarah Ferguson. When she herself married, she had wanted her as a lady-in-waiting, but she was considered too inexperienced: that she had taken up with a man old enough to be her father with two children cannot have helped her chances much either. The Princess of Wales greatly enjoyed her company, both had the same, 'giggly' sense of humour. She was also a great ally in what is one of the Princess of Wales's favourite pastimes, shopping. When Sarah Ferguson's three-year affair ended, 'Cupid' sprang into action to help her two friends. It worked, eventually, for them all.

Here, at last, was a friend at Court, an ally who would be around all the time during the royal migrations to Windsor, Sandringham, and Balmoral, with possibly the Royal Yacht thrown in as well. It is no accident that the expression 'friends and relations' is put that way round: you can choose your friends, but not your relations. As with any family, the Princess of Wales is closer to some members of the family than others, but there is no substitute for friends of your own choosing. There are, of course, other friends at Court, members of the Household who are always on hand, but, like her pre-wedding friends, they all bow or curtsey and call her Ma'am. Between royalty and commoners, however close a friendship, it is still a 'them and us' situation. A prime example is Alexandra Lloyd, the daughter of the Queen's land agent at Sandringham, whom the Princess has appointed as one of her extra ladies-in-waiting. The two girls grew up together, have known each other all their lives, and are still the greatest of friends. Now that the Princess of Wales is Her Royal Highness, her friend should not greet or leave her without curtseying, nor call her anything other than Ma'am, at least in public. Being Royal, the Duchess of York, of course, has no such barrier.

Apart from making two people she cares about happy, a great advantage of having Sarah Ferguson as a sister-in-law is that not only does she have a friend and an ally, but also a confidante. It works both ways too. They can unwind together, a mini-group therapy session. Both have the same pressures, in varying degrees. Both experience the same problems and doubts, things that those born to it would not experience, nor have had bred into them. But that was in the future.

When Sarah Ferguson left her secretarial college in London, the school's confidential assessment ran:

> Bright, bouncy redhead. She's a bit slapdash. But has initiative and personality which she will well use to her advantage when she gets older. Accepts responsibility happily.

A prophetic view of one still quite young. But it is just those very qualities that make her so ideal a wife for the Duke of York. He was to recognise them too. Although a far cry from the lithe former girlfriends, she is undeniably attractive. She is great fun and is very funny. They share the same kind of humour, mostly of the bread-roll-throwing, apple-pie-bed variety. But she is also very good for him. Just a few months older, she is far more mature than him. Beneath that bouncy exterior, is a true 'motherly' soul with just the right sensitivity to cope with the 'lost little boy' aspect of her husband. She also has the personality, strength to cope with, and indeed curb, his less attractive side, generally born out of 'royal schizophrenia'. One moment he was royal with his mother as Queen, the next a simple serving officer of junior rank, the next the young trendy in an *avant garde* nightclub like Tramp. She could easily divert a potentially pompous situation.

As with his great-grandfather, he liked to run with the hare and hunt with the hounds. Edward VII (as Prince of Wales) goodnaturedly rebuked a friend, Sir Frederick Johnstone, late at night with 'Freddy, Freddy, you're very drunk', to which, Sir Frederick, pointing to his host's stomach and imitating his rolling 'r's', replied 'Tum, Tum, you are ve*rrr*y fat!' He left before breakfast the next morning. The royal dignity had been offended. Prince Andrew staying at Floors Castle behaved in much the same way when, playing 'sardines' (a children's game where one person hides and is joined by the rest of the players who squeeze into the hiding place, like sardines in a tin). There is no winner, just a loser. When Sarah Ferguson found him under the table, she lifted the tablecloth and pinched his bottom to be told that she was not at liberty to pinch the royal bottom, yet.

Once again, the 'Palace gatherers' flocked to Buckingham Palace on the news of the engagement of Prince Andrew to Sarah Ferguson: once again, the whole Royal 'industry' leapt into action with its three-pronged attack. The astrologers worked out their respective astrological charts while the press and genealogists went to work on her family.

By contrast to the aristocratic Spencers, the genealogists found the origins of the Ferguson family to be perfectly respectable, but relatively undistinguished, and to be thoroughly middle-class from Belfast in Northern Ireland. The Fergusons were mostly of the professional class, doctors and, more recently, the military: Major Ronald Ferguson, Sarah Ferguson's father, being the fourth member of his family to serve in the Life Guards. The family was considerably socially elevated with various forays into the aristocracy, marriages that caused considerable excitement to the pundits who were thus able to trace her descent from various of Charles II's mistresses. Thus, without too much delving, they discovered that Sarah Ferguson and the Princess of Wales were fourth cousins.

While genealogists and astrologers were indulging in their harmless trades, the hunt was on by the tabloid press to find a 'past' for Sarah Ferguson. Where it was the Prince of Wales's 'duty' to provide the public, as one biographer put it, 'with perfection', there were no such strictures for his younger brother. Unlike the Princess of Wales, they did not have to muck-rake far to come up with two past lovers, who, with perfect manners, declined to give anything but the blandest statements on their liaisons. For a girl of twenty-six, it would have been newsworthy if she had *not* had the odd relationship, but such revelations merely enhanced her popularity with the public, at least with a public that was interested in the subject.

One feature that marked, rather marred, the months before the Princess of Wales's wedding was the unrelenting attention of the world's press; so bad did it become that the Queen had to call the editors of Fleet Street and ask them to desist. Mrs Shand Kydd wrote to *The Times* complaining at the treatment of her daughter, while questions were even asked in the House of Commons. She had suffered in the weeks leading up to the announcement of the engagement and, even with the security offered by the Palace staff after the official announcement, they were still to persecute her relentlessly (she once left a polo match in tears). She was, however, partially helped through those weeks, particularly on the polo ground (a semi-public place), by her friend Sarah Ferguson. When it was Sarah Ferguson's turn, she met with the same problem, but was able to cope much better. For a start, she was seven years older than the nineteen-year-old Lady Diana Spencer in the same predicament. She was worldly wise; she had visited her mother and stepfather, Hector Barrantes, in the Argentine and then travelled by local bus on to Rio de Janeiro, followed by a trip through the United States before returning to England and a succession of jobs. These jobs, like flat-letting or working in a fine art gallery, meant that she was continually meeting new people, of all nationalities, and class. With Lady Diana Spencer's job, she just met those same, upper-class mothers who sent their children to the nursery school where she was a helper. What stood Sarah Ferguson in good stead was her job with a public relations firm, Durden-Smith Communications. She was a seasoned professional at dealing with the press. Instead of blushing and hanging her head and saying nothing, like Lady Diana, Sarah Ferguson met them head on, beating them at their own game. When the 'rat-pack' (the tabloids' Royal watchers) pursued her to Antigua, she sent them over a bowl of flowers from her table: they responded by sending her a bottle of champagne. On the same trip, she called to photographers crouched behind some bushes waiting for a bikini-clad picture 'Don't get sunstroke, boys!'

That the Princess of Wales came through those early months as unscathed as she did, showed what she is made of. There was no one to follow (the Queen Mother was just comparable, but then she was sixty years out of date). At least when Sarah Ferguson followed her, she could advise her friend as no other member of the Royal Family could.

By the time Sarah Ferguson married, the pre-wedding television interview had become a tradition. Princess Anne, an old hand at television interviews anyway, had pulled Captain Mark Phillips painfully through what turned out to be an embarrassing ordeal. With the Prince and Princess of Wales, he did most of the talking, and when it drew to a close, it seemed a relief all round that it was over. In contrast, Prince Andrew and Sarah Ferguson's interview was a romp. It was only too evident that they were having the most jolly of times: slapping each other on the back like a couple of prep-school boys, he nearly knocking her off the wall into a flowerbed like some slapstick routine worthy of Laurel and Hardy: she with all the answers to delight the public – their interests in common and how she liked fish and chips (whitebait before literature). Where the Prince and Princess of Wales's concession to informality was to sit side by side on two upright, canvas chairs, gripping the arms, Prince Andrew and Sarah Ferguson could hardly keep their hands off each other.

Such comparisons are really unfair. Had the ages been reversed, the interviews would, of course, have come out very differently. At twenty-seven, the Princess of Wales is serene without being regal, polished but not over-sophisticated: the Duchess of York at twenty would doubtless have appeared just as gauche. In addition, in those five years between the two engagements and weddings, the beginning and the middle of the eighties, the public's view of the Royal Family, and what was expected of them, had radically altered, even in that short space of time.

The Expansion of the Monarchy

A dictionary definition of *honeymoon* reads 'holiday of newly married couple; initial period of enthusiasm or goodwill'. For the Princess of Wales and the Duchess of York, their honeymoons with their new spouses were over when they were disgorged from the Royal Yacht in the sun and deposited at a windswept Balmoral to be with the 'in-laws'. As far as the public was concerned, the latter type of honeymoon, at least for the Princess of Wales, would seemingly go on for ever.

When the public takes to someone, usually at the direction of the media, the chosen one is taken up whole heartedly. Such infatuation lasts for a limited period, while the film, the soap opera, the sport or whatever, is fashionable. Attention is then focussed on another, before the public has time to be bored with over-exposure of the first. However, when that person is also a member of the Royal Family, a different rule pertains: there must always be one member of the Royal Family in the news so that the interest in one member of the family will only fade when interest revives in another. The popular press are nothing if not fickle with their allegiance. The worldwide adoration of the Princess of Wales, and to a lesser extent, the interest in the Duchess of York, is hardly novel.

Before the advent of photographs in newspapers, that is before the First World War, the younger members of the Royal Family could walk about London with little fuss. If, by chance, anyone recognised them in the street, they merely acknowledged their presence by raising their hat or a slight curtsey, and politely continued on their way. After the War, the public wanted heroes, if not actual heroes, then heroic substitutes. The Prince of Wales [later Edward VIII] fitted neatly into the slot. He was popular, good looking and courageous (he hunted and steeplechased, though he rode badly). He appeared to care about the plight of the working class. He was gay, (in the old sense of the word), a perpetual party-goer and night-clubber. Some even followed him sartorially. He was always news: he epitomised the post-War hope of Britain, and the mood of the 'twenties, when youth conquered all. His filmstar popularity was to last virtually until he became King in 1936. When his brother, the Duke of York, married Lady Elizabeth Bowes-Lyon, the present Queen Elizabeth the Queen Mother, the public could not have enough of the 'smiling Duchess'. But the admiration that the public had for her then, as indeed the admiration she has commanded right up to the present day, was of a very dignified form, especially after the traumas of the Abdication, in her role as Queen Consort, particularly during the Second World War.

The Hollywood filmstars were already providing heroes and heroines for the public. But here was a different kind of star. These royal stars were, of course, far removed in life and style from ordinary people, but they could be seen in the flesh, and, most important of all, were British and not American. Where the Hollywood stars were idolised world wide for the parts they played, the enamoured actually wanted to *be* their idols; to talk like them, dress like them, live like them and so on. No one actually wanted to *be* the Prince of Wales, nor indeed *be* the Duchess of York, however much they admired them. The Royal Family were all unique individuals to be revered but not to be identified with. Television was to change all that. With the expansion of the media exposure of the Royal Family, it was only a matter of time before the same Hollywood principles would be applied to them. While that Prince of Wales and the Duchess of York were above such things, it was her daughter, Princess Elizabeth (the Queen) who became Britain's answer to Shirley Temple of the United States. The newspapers, magazines and newsreels were full of her: if she wore a yellow coat, then yellow coats became *de rigeur*. The sugary, royal biographer, Lady Cynthia Asquith asked her readers if there was a more celebrated child in the world than her, and speculated if 'even the most glittering film star has a wider circle of adorers than Princess Elizabeth'.[1] Her father, the Duke of York, once lamented: 'It worries me that people should love her so much.'

That juvenile start showed the shape of things to come. In 1934 the dashing Duke of Kent married Princess Marina of Greece. They made a handsome couple, or what 'Chips' Channon called 'a dazzling pair'. Here was the first member of the Royal Family with real 'star appeal'. She was descended from two royal houses, was beautiful, *soignée*, and extremely popular. For the first time, those from all walks of life who admired her emulated her. They copied her hairstyle, her clothes, her mannerisms in true Hollywood fashion. When Britain was emerging from the drab restrictions of the Second World War in the early 'fifties, it was the vivacious Princess Margaret who held the centre stage. After that, there was a lull until Princess Anne hit the headlines in the late 'sixties, early 'seventies. Again, a member of the Royal Family was seen to epitomise the spirit of a new decade, although in her case, the love affair was somewhat stormy and shortlived. Then, a whole decade later, a decade starved of a royal idol (Princess Michael did not even make it to the starting line, despite her glamour), came the Princess of Wales to bring in the 'eighties.

From the moment that the press had decided that Lady Diana Spencer was to marry the Prince of Wales (long before he did), they set her up on a pedestal; She became like the Henry James character 'famous for being famous'. This nineteen year-old girl could do no wrong. They reported her every move (and many, many more that she did not make) so that, virtually overnight, she became the best-known face in the world. She appeared in every newspaper and magazine from Alaska to Australia (the long way round), from Vienna to Valparaiso. Every editor soon learned, as indeed is still the case, the value of having her face smiling out of the front cover of a periodical or beneath some provocative headline on a paper. Certain tabloid sections of the media who claimed to have made her, also said that they could just as easily break her. Theirs was an idle boast as they found, six years later, when reporting the supposed breakdown of her marriage. Her fascination still knows no bounds.

In those early days she set a fashion; quite unintentionally, she became a trend-setter. Romance and romanticism were acceptable again. The 'Lady Di look' was in. Girls the world over dressed like her, the high street shops could not keep pace with the demand for 'pie-crust' collars and flat shoes; her haircut, the 'Lady Di' bob, was all the rage. 'Lady Di Lookalike' competitions were organised by every provincial paper. She engendered a pure cult following, a following on the lines of her royal predecessors, but with mega-star, Hollywood overtones. It was her as a person that they wanted to emulate, not her in her role as fiancée, (and later, wife) of the Prince of Wales, although it was that position, of course, that brought her the fame in the first place. In that, she has much in common with Princess Marina, Duchess of Kent, (right down to her engaging, lopsided smile). But the Princess of Wales was just being herself, little different from hundreds of other girls from similar backgrounds. She was a typical Sloane Ranger, a not-so-mythical character as delineated by Peter York in an article for *Harper's Queen*, of the lifestyle and happenings of a section of upper-class life. Those 'Sloanes' who could identify with Caroline and Henry, the two mythical protagonists, would not readily admit to their new sobriquet. To those who were not of their number, they were figures of fun. Either way, the article was widely received and the term went into the common usage.

Mrs Thatcher arrived at Number 10 Downing Street two years before Lady Diana Spencer arrived at Buckingham Palace. With her, eventually, came an expansion of the economy, and with that, a new opportunity to make money. This new money could buy what those old Sloane Rangers took for granted. Suddenly, everything was possible, regardless of origin. It was like the American dream come true; from log cabin to White House, or the soldier finding that there really was a Field Marshal's baton in his knapsack. The Sloane Rangers' lifestyle was no longer the exclusive preserve of the Sloanes themselves: equally, they were no longer figures of fun, but, for some, something to strive for. When Ann Barr and York brought out *The Official Sloane Ranger Handbook*, it sold hundreds of thousands of copies to Sloanes and prospective Sloanes alike. The Princess of Wales was naturally dubbed the 'Supersloane', and as such revered by her fellows. But to those would-be Sloanes, she represented far more: here was living proof of what the eighties were all about. Her transition from stately home to palace, was just the same as would-be Sloane to Sloane. And they all loved her for it. It was Princess Alexandra who once said in the sixties that 'nowadays we have to compete with Elizabeth Taylor and the Beatles'[2], but that was before the arrival of the Princess of Wales. The boot is now firmly on the other foot.

There is much more to the acclaim of the Princess of Wales and her sister-in-law, the Duchess of York, than, to put it in its most simplistic terms, being the latest 'royal pop idol' or the heroines of a 'pack of socially, upwardly mobiles'. Over the years, the monarchy has changed inwardly to keep pace with the times: the public's view of the monarchy has also changed, which is not, of course, the same thing at all. These two, new, royal additions fit neatly into the new pattern of things. As women, they also fit neatly into the old pattern of things: the monarchy as a matriachy. For the last 150 years, royal subjects have become 'used' to women in positions of power, either as Sovereign (Queen Victoria and the present Queen), or at least a dominant influence behind the monarch (the forceful Queen Mary and Queen Elizabeth the Queen Mother). Today, those same subjects are both ruled and governed by women. (After Mrs Thatcher's election to an unprecedented third term in office, a small boy asked, 'Daddy, can a man become Prime Minister?')

The Queen is Head of State, but the undisputed head of the Royal Family as a family is the Duke of Edinburgh. He has been both their severest critic and most loyal guardian. This family arbiter keeps its members up to the mark, and guards the Royal Family's image zealously. But the Duke is uniquely qualified to this self-appointed role. An outsider, he married into a rigid system that had altered little since the days of Queen Victoria. 'If it is good enough for my father, then it is good enough for me' was then very much the attitude, regardless of public opinion or what was going on inside the Palace portals. What is more, on her accession, the young Queen had inherited George VI's courtiers, in the main an intransigent lot, resistant to change. In that, there is a direct parallel to be drawn between George V after the First World War and the Queen. Both were also resistant to change; both stood for the old order of things, and were surrounded by a Court with whom they felt comfortable. But the twenties, like the fifties, was a period of post-war change. The Prince of Wales stood for the new order (with the inevitable conflict with the old order), and was universally popular. The Queen on her Accession was about the same age as the Prince of Wales was at the start of the decade, twenty-six, yet she, and her Court, still represented a 'fifties version of the 'old order'. That was all very well for her like-minded subjects, but hardly progressive, nor was it what was hoped for in the 'New Elizabethan Age'.

As a boy, the Duke of Edinburgh, then Prince Philip of Greece, had been brought up amongst the Royal houses of Europe. During those summer holidays with them, he had witnessed, first hand, the dangers of too rigid a system. He could see the value of change, not just for change's sake, but the need to change with the times:

Most of the Monarchies of Europe were really destroyed by their greatest and most ardent supporters. It was the most reactionary people who tried to hold onto something without letting it develop and change.[3]

He could see the problem, but, at that time, could do very little about it.

The mysticism of the monarchy, produced by the Coronation in 1953, soon began to fade. It was just not enough for the Queen to be, as Robert Lacy described her, an 'icon': the public wanted, and needed, the 'real thing', not just 'an image of a sacred person' as Sovereign. The Coronation had shown, through television, that there really was life behind the Palace railings, yet those same Palace railings insulated her from her subjects: not so much an ivory tower, but a far-off castle. In her efforts to keep her private life, especially her children, sacrosanct, she distanced herself from her people. She surrounded herself with a coterie of like-minded aristocrats (many were her father's friends and his exact contemporaries), those dedicated to the country and country pursuits, often out of touch with anything outside their own world. They were, in a word, 'insular'.

In her defence, the Queen had hardly known a life other than the one she chose to lead. Unlike her father and grandfather, George VI and George V, both second sons not destined to succeed to the throne, the Queen was brought up from the age of ten, consciously or subconsciously, as the Heir Presumptive. She led a protected life, educated at home (mostly through the War years) and met with only family and friends of her parents (and their children), members of the Household and the Palace staff. Both her father and grandfather were, for a period, serving Naval officers, mixing freely with others from all walks of life. George VI had a great understanding of his subjects, not least through his work on industrial relations and his boys' club camps drawn from every social class. The Buckingham Palace Brownie and Guide packs were hardly a substitute for that contact.

On the other side of the coin was the Duke of Edinburgh, open, outgoing, and very much his own man, working and acting independently from the Palace. For a time, this dual role worked:

one extrovert, one introvert. But the more the Queen guarded her private life, the more the public, through the media, wanted at least a glimpse of it: after all, here was a young Queen and a dashing husband with two children who *ought* to have been newsworthy, but was not. Without that human interest angle, the official face of Royalty was just dull, and nothing breeds indifference more than dullness.

There is no doubt that the tragic love affair of Princess Margaret and the divorced Group Captain Peter Townsend did tarnish the image of the monarchy, but not in the way that was envisaged by the Establishment who so opposed their marriage. They believed that had such a marriage taken place, it would irreparably damage the standing of the Crown. They were not to find out. Princess Margaret made a heart-rending decision and declared that she would not marry Peter Townsend. Although the Establishment, the old-fashioned courtiers and the Tory Cabinet (who were faced with a possible revolt), were delighted, the general sympathy was with the Princess. In a poll in October 1955, 59 per cent of the population were in favour of the marriage, and only 17 per cent actively disapproved. Of that 17 per cent, only half were against the match because Townsend was divorced. 'The typing pool at Morgan's Crucible Works is simply seething. They all think that she ought to have married him'.[4] To most, she was a martyr to a succession of outdated Acts of Parliament and a hidebound system. But she did show that there was a human face of Royalty, and that they were ordinary mortals with human feelings too.

Another outcome of the Townsend affair was the part played by the press. Foreign newspapers had been speculating on the affair for months, finally to be followed by the British press. For the first time, the trials and anguish of a member of the Royal Family were laid bare and discussed quite openly by the media; some from a constitutional viewpoint, the majority as a human interest story. They soon found the mileage to be had from royal gossip. They extended it to every possible area of the Royal Family. The Palace Press Office either ignored their claims, or occasionally issued a denial. When the denial was picked up, it was made into yet another story. But these attacks on the Royal Family were not confined to the tabloid press.

A swingeing article on the Queen and her Court came from Lord Altrincham. Writing what was intended as constructive criticism, in the August 1957 edition of his *National and English Review*, he took the Queen to task over her debutante image of 'Crawfie [the governess], the London Season, the race-course, Canasta, and the occasional royal tour'. He branded her friends as 'almost without exception the "tweedy" sort', while her Courtiers had:

> lamentably failed to live with the times. While the Monarchy has become popular and multi-racial, the Court has remained a tight little enclave of English ladies and gentlemen[5]

He accused them, particularly her speech writer, of stultifying the Queen:

> The personality conveyed by the utterances which are put into her mouth is that of a priggish schoolgirl, captain of the hockey team, a perfect and a recent candidate for confirmation.

The effect was electric, even painful for Altrincham who was slapped by a member of the League of Empire Loyalists after a television interview with Robin Day. The Establishment denounced him as a 'bounder', thought he should be 'hanged, drawn and quartered', while the good burghers of Altrincham declared that 'No town has a greater sense of loyalty to the Crown than the Borough of Altrincham'.[6] Despite the loyal outbursts, the *Daily Mail* found to its horror in a poll they commissioned, that the majority of their younger readers actually agreed with Altrincham. Six years later, when he renounced his title, he blamed the storm on the 'Shintoistic atmosphere of the post-Coronation period ... there was a tendency, quite alien to our national tradition ... to regard as high treason any criticism of the monarch, however loyal and constructive its intent'.[7]

Malcolm Muggeridge, the former editor of *Punch* and something of a television cult figure, also offered up a study of the

Royal Family, writing in the *Saturday Evening Post*. It was he who coined the term 'royal soap opera', likening them to 'a sort of substitute or ersatz religion'.[8] His article was widely reported, but worse, it was paraphrased by the *Sunday Express* and the *People* giving it a totally different meaning. He, like Altrincham, had meant to be constructive in his analysis, instead he was pilloried for being disloyal. John Osborne, who made a profession of being an angry young man, had no such thoughts when declaring in the intellectual magazine, *Encounter*, that the Royal symbol was dead '... a gold filling in a mouth full of decay'. He found the whole system anachronistic:

> It bores me, it distresses me that there should be so many empty minds, so many empty lives in Britain to sustain this fatuous industry. ... When the mobs rush forward in the Mall, they are taking part in the last circus of civilisation that has lost faith in itself and has sold itself for a splendid triviality.[9]

However well-meaning, or otherwise, these seeds of dissension were, they can only have been distressing for those members of the Royal Family, and doubtless cause for concern for those 'tweedy ladies and gentlemen' who were in the direct firing line. But such onslaughts did have some effect, whether directly or indirectly (or was it merely coincidentally?), when certain changes were implemented to soften the austere image of the monarchy. The Queen began her lunches at Buckingham Palace, at which she had met a far wider cross section of the community than she had ever met before. At those lunches, as indeed today, she and other members of the Royal Family, talk informally with a huge variety of guests, captains of industry, actors, watch-makers, social workers or whoever. At that time, 1957, presentations at Court were ended. Presentations had become somewhat of a farce by then anyway, when the only criteria for being there was that the debutante's mother, or relation, had been presented before, or the family had enough money to pay for a professional who could do it for them. Life peerages were introduced which meant that women could sit in the House of Lords. Another innovation, particularly for a family labelled as philistines, was the plan to rebuild the bombed chapel at Buckingham Palace as an art gallery to show off the Royal collection.

What was to have a far-reaching effect on the public was the televising of the Queen's Speech on Christmas Day. As those early broadcasts were live, it was a tremendous ordeal for one who felt unconfident about her ability to cope with the cameras. As a Courtier put it: 'Television in the Queen's opinion is an uncongenial medium: she doesn't believe that she will ever be able to talk to the camera like an old friend'.[10] It was a great innovation, and success. Harold Nicolson was impressed, writing: 'She came across quite clear, and with a vigour unknown in pre-Altrincham days'.[11] But the Queen was very much her own woman, resolutely refusing to pander to the demands of the press. She was not interested in presenting an image, merely in being herself, a factor common to all members of the Royal Family. Press reports, particularly wildly exaggerated fiction concocted by the foreign press, were for amusement, not for study. The Queen would not change on demand, but certain events within the Royal Family did considerably bolster the royal image. The public's attitude to the Royal Family was changing too, from affectionate deference to unbridled curiosity.

The news of Princess Margaret's engagement to Antony Armstrong-Jones was greeted with genuine enthusiasm. Here, at last, the Princess had found happiness; that she had chosen a commoner, a working photographer, complete with the name of Jones, came as even better news. The news marginally preceded the birth of the Queen's third child, Prince Andrew, in February 1960, which re-kindled the human interest side of the monarchy. (Even then, there were no photographs of the baby for six months until he appeared on the Queen Mother's lap for her official sixtieth birthday portrait.) Apart from the few predictable carpings about the cost, the wedding of the popular Princess and her commoner was a huge success, with all the trappings of State and the usual Walter Bagehot quotes on princely marriages uniting mankind. The wedding of Princess Alexandra and the Honourable Alexander Ogilvy, and the birth of the Queen's fourth child, Prince Edward, were greeted with good, solid patriotic fervour, but after Princess Margaret's wedding and the birth of Prince Andrew, it was all slightly *déjà vu*.

But no number of royal babies – apart from the Queen's 'second' family, Princess Margaret, the Duchess of Kent and Princess Alexandra produced 8 between them in the space of five years – could compensate for the steady tarnishing of the Royal image throughout the sixties. There were the 'own goals', unfortunate mistakes that could so easily have been avoided. Photographs of the Queen and Prince Philip appeared in the press with the tiger he had shot; a rare white rhinoceros was shot by one of their party. Up to 1965 it was the monarch who invited the Prime Minister of their choice to form a Government. The choice of Lord Home to succeed Harold Macmillan as Prime Minister, had all the hallmarks of the appointment of Macmillan when he succeeded Anthony Eden. However able they were thought to be for that position, the appointment smacked of Her Majesty's preference for the 'tweedy' country gentleman. Even the tenth anniversary of the Coronation passed virtually unnoticed. The National Anthem was rarely heard in cinemas and theatres. Throughout the 'sixties', there was nothing royal to get excited about. Perhaps Malcolm Muggeridge was right when he said 'the English are getting bored with their Monarchy'[12], a cry taken up, uncharacteristically, by *The Sunday Telegraph* who observed:

> a marked change in the public's attitude towards the Crown. Most people cared much less than they did – particularly the young, many of whom regard the Queen as the arch-square. They are not *against* in the sense of being *for a* republic. They are quite simply indifferent . . .[13]

As in all good fairy stories, things have to get worse before they can get better, and fifteen years after the Coronation, the reign must have touched its lowest ebb. Then 'spake the voice from within', the Duke of Edinburgh in an interview in Canberra in 1967: 'No one wants to end up like a brontosaurus, who couldn't adapt himself, and ended up stuffed in a museum . . . it isn't exactly where I want to end up myself.[14] If the Duke of Edinburgh could not be seen to adapt the system, he could at least orchestrate that adaptation from the wings.

The break came with the gradual introduction of a new set of enlightened men into the Household. A significant appointment was that of William Heseltine, a personable Australian, as Assistant Press Secretary to the Queen (under the inflexible, old-guard Commander Colville). Heseltine, now the Queen's Private Secretary, spent a year on secondment from his position as Private Secretary to the Australian Prime Minister, Sir Robert Menzies, in the Press Office at Buckingham Palace in 1960. It was the Duke of Edinburgh's idea to lure him back so he could take over when Colville retired, which he did in 1968. Another appointment to the Household was David Checketts, who came as the Prince of Wales's equerry.

It distressed these two intelligent 'outsiders' to see the yawning gap between how the Royal Family really were, and how they appeared to the public. This discrepancy, particularly with the Prince of Wales, had not gone unnoticed by others either. According to John Pearson in his *Ultimate Family*, Checketts was approached by a wartime acquaintance, Nigel Neilson, the head of a successful public relation's firm, Neilson McCarthy, based in Mayfair (two of its directors were Jack di Manio and the Duchess of York's father, Major Ronald Ferguson).

Neilson could see the value of the young Prince of Wales and the damage that was being done to him by the media:

> Here was a first class chap, a first class product, being criminally undersold. Far too much nonsense in the press about the chinless wonder, and his ears that are no different from anybody else's. So I decided something must be done.[15]

What he did was to make Checketts a non-executive director of Neilson McCarthy at a nominal salary. That way Checketts could sit in on meetings and learn their 'craft' by association. Further, there was a ready, and free, source of advice when needed

The 'propitiation' of the Princess of Wales on her visit to Germany.

The caring faces of monarchy – the Prince and
Princess of Wales visit the flood victims in Wales.

The Princess of Wales personally attended the
memorial service for victims of the fire at King's
Cross Underground Station.

A young admirer's gift to the Duchess of York on her visit to Northern Ireland.

Positively regal, the Princess of Wales in her Tudor evening dress.

Despite her extensive jewellery collection, the Princess likes to mix 'real' with 'costume'.

The Duchess of York arriving at Sadler's Wells, March 1987, wearing a stunning velvet gown complete with feathers and bows.

The latest in aviation chic.

A novel departure from the
Princess's sartorial norm.

'The Waleses' on holiday with the King and Queen of Spain in Majorca.

The matriarchal monarchy – the Queen and Queen Mother with the Princess of Wales outside Clarence House before lunch on the Queen Mother's 87th birthday.

Every wife and child knows a life by the side of the ground with a polo-playing husband and father.

Keep it in the family – the Prince of Wales after receiving his prize from his sister-in-law at the Guard's Polo Club.

on any specific problem. The effect was immediate. The media were actually encouraged to take an interest in the burgeoning Prince: two drinks parties were arranged for the press so that they could actually meet him. The gamble paid off, as they knew it would, and with the new, improved relations between Palace and press, the Prince of Wales was firmly established as the rising star of the Royal Family. His confidence grew with his success. Carefully briefed and rehearsed, he gave an interview for the *Today* programme with Jack di Manio. Other radio and television interviews followed, all successful and firmly showing the advantages of the proper 'packaging' of the young Prince. He had become a 'hot property', proven and popular. But that was only the shape of things to come.

It was all a matter of timing. Heseltine had taken over from Colville as Press Secretary, when David Frost approached him to make a documentary for ITV about Prince Charles to coincide with the Investiture. Lord Brabourne, who had just made a documentary about the life and times of his father-in-law, Earl Mountbatten of Burma, which had been well received within the family, suggested that it was time for something similar for the rest of the family. The result was the making of *Royal Family*, a documentary 110 minutes long, filmed by the BBC.

The film showed the family for what they were: a hard-working, sensible, and wholly devoted family. It showed them working, and at 'play'; it gave a hitherto, unseen view of that sacred private life at Balmoral. Above all, it achieved just what it set out to do, to show the 'human face of Royalty'. The film was judged a huge success with peak audience figures when screened on both television channels. At a stroke, the Royal Family's 'ratings' went up immeasurably: the public seemed to better understand what the monarchy was all about. The Audience Research Report held that:

The norm is for broadcasts to reinforce existingly held opinions. The fact that changes *did* occur, suggests that some of those who chose to view the film had attitudes towards her

Majesty which were seen to be 'incorrect' (in the light of the
information that the film provided that a new and different
image was adopted.[16]

Coming out just before the Investiture, the timing of the film
was also significant. On one hand the public witnessed that the
Royal Family were indeed real people, then they saw them at their
most formal and hierarchical, a reminder that there was still a
'mystery about the Crown, a religious and spiritual significance
that transcended the constitutional or social sphere'.[17] It was all
a masterpiece of planning, a marriage of public relations and
progressiveness of the new members of the Household presenting
a highly professional family for what they were and, more important, what they stood for. The Palace shutters had been drawn
back to reveal a closeknit, and contented, family, one which the
public (should they so wish) could relate to, either individually
or as a whole. But once they had transcended from their symbolic
role to one of 'super-stars', they could never again retreat behind
the Palace shutters.

Seven years before, Harold Nicolson wrote:

> Too much publicity will strain the mystery, even the dignity
> of the Crown. Too little publicity will be regarded as undemo-
> cratic and will render the gulf that yawns between the sovereign
> and the ordinary subject an unfortunate barrier rather than a
> necessity of segregation.[18]

The argument for and against the democratisation of the Royal
Family went on and on (as indeed, it is still a constant subject
today). Milton Shulman asked:

> Is it, in the long run, wise for the Queen's advisers to set as a
> precedent this right of the television camera to act as an image-
> making apparatus for the monarchy? Every institution that has
> so far attempted to use TV to popularise or aggrandise itself,
> has been trivialised by it.[19]

Peregrine Worsthorne thought that William Heseltine had gone
too far in creating this new 'look' to the Royal Family:

So successful have the modernisers been in turning the Royal Family into human beings that they seem increasingly ill-at-ease on the occasions when they have to be what they are primarily intended to be: symbols of authority and majesty.

The great British public wanted to have their cake and to eat it. While they generally enjoyed the revelation of seeing the Royal Family as they really were behind the scenes, opinion polls suggested that they were still expected to be the embodiment of those 'symbols of authority and majesty', and all that goes with it. However, for the rest of the public, largely fed by the media, the new openness of the Royal Family was preferable to the old, closed order. Right or wrong, they were at least prepared for the new decade, the seventies, and, more important, they were not to be relegated to a museum, as feared by the Duke of Edinburgh. Although still very much a united family, they were now all treated as individual characters. Before, if something, good or bad, exciting or bland, happened to one member of the family, it reflected on the whole family. Afterwards, as individuals, it was each to their own. So, when Princess Anne was criticised for lambasting photographers (rightly) when they upset her horse at some horse trials, it did not affect the standing of the Queen. Likewise, when Princess Anne won the European Championship, she took the credit and not 'Royal Family Inc.'. That said, family occasions, like her marriage to Captain Mark Phillips, were seen as a happy family occasion shared with a huge, television audience; the criticism of their unfortunate interview before the wedding, however, was aimed at her alone. The same could be said of the breakdown of Princess Margaret's marriage. There were those who used the divorce as a vehicle to attack the monarchy, but the majority of criticism, unfairly, was for her alone.

The Queen's Silver Jubilee in 1977 showed that the process of the democratisation of the Royal Family started nearly a decade ago with the film *Royal Family* was complete. The build up to the Jubilee was slow. The Queen began her famous 'walkabouts', something the Queen Mother had pioneered so many years before, but only then adopted by her daughter. By the actual day, 7 June, the whole country was united, not for one of Walter Bagehot's princely weddings, but in a passionate display of loyalty to the Sovereign. It was that same display of genuine affection which the country had shown for her grandfather, George v. During his Silver Jubilee summer, he was amazed at his popularity. 'I didn't realise they felt like this,' he said. They felt like that for the Queen too: when she passed the crowd on the way to the Guildhall, a secretary told her, 'We have come here because we love you,' to which the Queen replied, 'I can feel it, and it means so much to me.' Such affection was not just for the Queen as Monarch, but for the Queen herself, no longer seen as the divine person or 'icon' at her Coronation, but as a very real person, a wife and a mother (and grandmother too of Master Peter Phillips). Ramsay MacDonald wrote of George v's popularity, 'With it all, he retains the demeanour and status of King': the same could have been written of the Queen forty years later.

This dual position of the Queen, so ably demonstrated at her Silver Jubilee, confirmed, once and for all, the direction of the Monarchy. It was a brilliant juxtaposing of the roles. Through television and her Royal visits throughout Great Britain and Northern Ireland (and the Commonwealth) she, and other members of the Royal Family, had become even better known. Like the Indian rope trick, if you had not actually seen, or met, a member of the Royal Family, then you knew somebody who knew somebody who had. But with all this exposure, they lost nothing of that mystique of Royalty that had been 'bred' into them over the the centuries. While retaining something of an awesome presence, they still come across as 'awfully nice' people; though with no actual power, they still enjoy all the trappings associated with the monarchy: prestige, grandeur, wealth, privileged lifestyle, and, above all, presence. The virtual over-exposure of the Royal Family at that time did nothing to lessen its appeal, but rather to enhance it in the true, fairy-tale tradition; the better known the story, the more popular it becomes.

The public having become increasingly familiar with the Royal

Family through the media, they not unnaturally became a 'cast of characters'. If, because of their regal background they were not readily identifiable, then they were compared to others as 'seen on TV'. or, to go back to the fairy-tale analogy, the characters in the story. So each member took a role. In order for the 'goodies' to be good, so there must be 'baddies'. There were ample members of the Royal Family to fill each role: the Queen and Queen Elizabeth the Queen Mother for the former, and, in the eyes of the press, Princess Margaret and Princess Anne for the latter. However, the only ingredient lacking amongst that 'cast' was glamour, but, as in the best, traditional fairy-tale mode, glamour had to be good.

Princess Michael of Kent, when added to that cast of characters in 1978, might have filled the bill. She was undeniably glamorous and did much to bolster the somewhat flagging standing of her husband. However, as a consummate actress, she did not fit neatly into the pattern of the Royal Family. The Royal Family are universally good performers, all gifted amateurs with varying amounts of acting talent. But they are not 'acting' when they are 'performing', either in public and certainly not in private, they are just being themselves. When Malcolm Muggeridge coined the expression 'Royal Soap Opera' in 1956 he was certainly wide of the mark even then. However, twenty years on, Princess Michael, with her jet-set life and shadowy past, did fit neatly into that slot. It was not long before she, despite her undoubted intelligence and glitzy style, was named 'Princess Pushy' by the press, and so destined to join the 'baddies'. Her departure meant that there was still a vacancy for a glamorous 'goody'.

The longer the role remained unfilled, the more it was thought to be needed. Not before time, the media ceased to hound Princess Margaret. Also long overdue was the media's treatment of Princess Anne, later to be given the title of Princess Royal by the Queen. It was not until the 'rat-pack' followed her to Bakino Fasso, West Africa, that they actually appreciated her work. They had gone ostensibly to pick up some gossip on the state of her marriage. Instead they found the hard-working President of the

Save the Children Fund, travelling in great discomfort on her morale-boosting, fact-finding mission. They were amazed at her knowledge, at her compassion, and her wit. They returned a chastened bunch with the true picture, never again to bring up the boring old chestnut of the state of her marriage. Despite the *volte-face* by the press on the Princess, this mother-of-two could not seriously be thought of in the glamorous role.

That role of 'glamour' within the Royal Family, was, as indeed it is today, filled by the Princess of Wales. She is supported, to a lesser extent, by the Duchess of York. Her arrival in Royal circles makes the 'story' complete: as a bibliographical analogy, she was the final volume to complete a set of rare and valuable books. In this case, each volume is an entity in its own right, but, with the addition of the last, the set is more valuable, and as such is prized more than its value on its own (particularly if that particular volume was a long time in the finding).

But much more is, of course, required of the Princess of Wales in filling that role of 'glamour'. She is undoubtedly more than just a pretty face; the Royal Family more than a set of books (an ever-expanding part-work might be a closer analogy). That both the Princess and the Duchess of York (as will the future Prince Edward), had to *become* royal and play their part as such in the unfolding saga is, without doubt, the hardest part of their role. As neither was born royal, becoming a member of the Royal Family overnight puts them in danger of merely acting out the part (a problem not encountered by Lord Snowdon, Mark Phillips or the Hon Angus Ogilvy, none of whom became royal on marriage). The appeal of the Royal Family is that dual role of appearing 'ordinary' and royal at the same time. For the two newcomers, they could certainly satisfy the former, and only develop the latter in time.

Princesses for Sale

'The British royal family is an adman's dream, a unique selling proposition with a pliable market strongly predisposed towards the product'[1] Although even the thought of 'marketing' the Royal Family like some consumer product is a total anathema to the Royal Family, and particularly the Household, likening them to a highly successful 'product' is an interesting notion, particularly where the Princess of Wales and the Duchess of York are concerned. In fact, examining them, commoners turned Royal, in such a light, goes a long way to explaining their enduring, worldwide appeal and their popularity. The observation was even prophetic, in that the hypothesis is even truer today than when written nearly twenty years ago.

The product and image characteristics of the two brands, the *Princess of Wales* and the *Duchess of York*, could hardly be more different, yet they are marketed in exactly the same way. They appeal (or not), to the same market sectors. In their own way, each satisfies the overlapping psychological/physiological needs of that market, (that is, either as an example to, or being identifiable with, that audience). As the two women are now members of the same 'family firm' (as George VI called the Royal Family), they are automatically newsworthy, and therefore the subjects of an instant audience, while both stand out well in comparison with the direct, and indirect competition. But first one must define the products themselves through their key characteristics (that is, the salient points of their characters, appearance and lifestyle), and to compare the one with the other.

No one, least of all herself, could possibly describe the Princess of Wales as being an intellectual; her 'tweedy' background and genteel schools saw to that, even if, in the unlikely event, those seeds were there to be germinated in the first place. On the other hand, the Duchess of York who had a similar, country upbringing and B-stream schooling, while not being over-educated, does have a certain native wit. Having done so much more than the Princess of Wales before she married, she is undeniably 'street-wise' and it shows ... while the Princess went to Verbier to ski with a party of chums staying in a chalet, Sarah Ferguson has lived and travelled to the full. In direct contrast, with her secure and privileged life and her romantic, princely notions since the age of fifteen or sixteen, it is not surprising that the Princess of Wales should find herself, then as now, in an ivory tower, or dream world. Against this fairy-tale existence, the Duchess of York is thoroughly down to earth, if not downright earthy. She had no such early thoughts of marrying Prince Andrew (very much the reverse: when he did propose she thought it might have been a joke).

Not only do they differ in character and outlook, but in the way they are perceived by the public and also their friends. Whereas the Princess of Wales is permanently set on her pedestal, the Duchess of York has her feet firmly on the ground. Being pedestal-bound, the Princess of Wales is often isolated from her old friends. Those friends whom she does keep up with, she generally sees for lunch, or when dining with mutual friends, more often it is by letter. The Princess of Wales relies heavily on her family, especially her sister Lady Jane Fellowes, her neighbour in Kensington Palace and at their family home, Althorp, where the Fellowes have a farmhouse on the estate and she has the use of a flat in the house.

The Duchess of York, however, has no such constraints. She has the freedom of choice, not just with her friends but, within reason, her lifestyle as well. As with most marriages, friends and acquaintances from both sides are whittled down to provide a new nucleus of mutual friends. The Duchess, being an exact contemporary of her husband, with similar interests and humour, has been able to keep up with most of her old friends, as well as adding to that mutual nucleus. It is also a great deal easier for the Duke of York to visit his father-in-law, than the Prince of Wales to visit his. Where the Princess is remote, the Duchess is accessible.

The Princess of Wales comes across as feminine, passive but often unadventurous. In a large, public gathering, there is often the frightened greyhound look about her, a complete contrast to the hyperactive Duchess of York. Where a typical view of the Princess is of her demurely shopping or leading one of her children on his small pony, the Duchess of York is all dare-devil, leaping out of aeroplanes and helicopters, on the back of Aldaniti the Grand National winner in a sponsored ride. She has the air of a Lady Bounciful, a perpetual team leader in 'The Grand Knockout Tournament' (see page 121). Where the Princess appears somewhat brittle, the Duchess comes across as a 'toughy'. The Princess would never have canoed down the Hanbury River in Canada like her sister-in-law, not because it might appear unseemly, but because she is, quite simply, not interested in physically demanding pastimes.

These two women are as near the same age as makes no difference, yet they are already at very different stages of their lives. By the time the Princess of Wales was twenty-three, she had already achieved the most important role of her princely marriage: she had produced not only the heir, Prince William, but the 'spare' as well. Her next important role, that of becoming Queen, is, *DV*, far in the future (the last two Princesses of Wales, Queen Mary and Queen Alexandra were 43 and 57 respectively before their husbands succeeded). If the Queen reaches her mother's present age, the Princess of Wales will be 52. For one still young, her husand's succession can only appear far distant.

Thus, having achieved her first goal young, and the next not being in the foreseeable future, there is, apart from her children, the odd charity and official function, little of major importance to look forward to in her life. With nothing immediate to anticipate, the only alternative is to become retrospective, even introspective. The Duchess of York, on the other hand, has everything to look forward to. And so she should, married for just two years and expecting her first child in August.

To give these sisters-in-law a fictional analogy, the Duchess of York is pure 'Tigger', that bouncy character created by A. A. Milne in *The House at Pooh Corner*: 'a friendly Tigger, a Grand Tigger, a large and Helpful Tigger, a Tigger who bounced . . . in just the beautiful way a Tigger ought to bounce'.[2] The Princess of Wales, on the other hand, is a natural Cinderella.

The adman would see his 'dream' another way. Here are these two brands, the *Princess of Wales* and the *Duchess of York*: one remote, set on her pedestal in an ivory tower, the other streetwise, down to earth and accessible. Likening them to chocolates (soap powders would hardly be appropriate here) the *Princess of Wales* brand is an indulgence, very expensive, and beautifully packaged as a gift for a special occasion. Inside the box, the few chocolates (bitter chocolate, no less, an acquired taste) are flecked with gold leaf, the liqueur filling in the fragile case, cast in the shape of some exotic shell. The *Duchess of York* brand of chocolates (despite the nomenclature, *not* a Yorkie Bar), is expensive, but not impossible to buy for yourself. The packaging is practical, possibly with a re-useable box. Essentially, they are for sharing. The box is crammed full of small, individual plain chocolate *batonières*, which is fortunate, as they prove to be popular. There are enough to go round.

On paper, the Duchess of York with all her easy-going attributes should be the brand leader, but the opinion polls show very much the reverse. On examination, it is not difficult to see why. After the showing of the film *Royal Family*, it was feared that some of the mystique of the monarchy would be lost. One critic, the anthropologist David Attenborough, in recalling what he had observed in primitive societies, spoke ominously of the troubles that ensued when tribesmen broke the old rules and peered 'at the tribal mysteries inside the headsman's hut'.[3] The *Sunday Dispatch* asked if their readers would like to meet the Queen out shopping or the Duke of Edinburgh on the underground or would they prefer to keep the 'Queen and her family just that little bit more remote from everybody else?'.[4] The public consensus then was for the latter, they were all for the 'mystique of the monarchy'.

Part of the 'suitability' of the Princess of Wales was that she was so young, with all the freshness of youth but without firmly fixed ideas of her own. She was pliable and could be moulded by design or association to become a royal clone. The Duchess of York, on the other hand, being that much older when she married, had very fixed ideas of her own, and an established pattern of behaviour. She is totally herself, and commendable for that too. They are like the difference between *haute couture* or bespoke and 'off the peg'. Thus, the Princess of Wales, remote and in her ivory tower (which is not the same thing as being aloof), fits exactly into the public's demand for that mystique in the monarchy. It is that controlled distancing that is preferable in the end, not the ebullient Lady Bounciful.

The institution of monarchy is an integral part of Britain's heritage. The Princess of Wales, as the mother of the future king, has become a part custodian of that heritage. The Duchess of York, however, plays a lesser role as custodian because, though her children will be royal, their children, the Duke's and Duchess's grandchildren, will not.

The two sisters-in-law became instant public figures the very moment their names were coupled with that of their husbands, and so they will remain until they die. Possibly what they did not bargain for was that they would become public property as well — historically, however remote the monarch has been, they have always been referred to as *our* king or *our* queen. 'God save our gracious Queen' as in the National Anthem. As in the proverbial fairy tale, the better known they become, the more they are wanted. They, especially the Princess of Wales, have become a never ending source of 'fodder' for the media, both at home, and particularly abroad, with the increased sales a photograph of the Princess of Wales on the cover brings. When, in 1968, the press was invited to take an interest in the young Prince Charles and asked them to assign a reporter exclusively to him, the idea was met with bemused indifference. Today, the tabloids have done just that, although the 'Rat-Pack' delve into their private life as opposed to reporting their public works. They say that they are satisfying an insatiable demand for news of them which, in one way, is true, but an dreadful nuisance for the protagonists.

As integral members of the Royal Family, the Princess of Wales and the Duchess of York are seen as an important part of that huge industry, Great Britain Ltd. At home, they do their share of public works and charities – charity organisers well know the benefits of having one of the Royal Family as a patron, particularly as is the trend today when they take an active part, rather than merely lending their name. Abroad, unless it is working for a worldwide charity like the Princess Royal and the Save the Children Fund, or the Duke of Edinburgh and the World Wildlife Fund, the Royal Family, including the sisters-in-law, are seen by the responsible as Great Britain Ltd's ambassadors of good will, with all the benefits of trade and commerce that go with their visits. To the *papparazzi*, however, they are little more than perpetual film stars, and are treated as such. The same is true in America, where they are truly 'star-oriented'. On both Continents, both are mega-stars. When *People Weekly*, the American periodical that covers the happenings of the rich and famous, had to choose which bride to feature on the front cover of the magazine, the future Duchess of York or Caroline Kennedy (daughter of the late President and Jacqueline Onassis, the nearest to a homegrown princess in the United States), they chose the Duchess for the main cover and had a small inset for Miss Kennedy.

Opinion polls have shown that the public (those 'strongly predisposed towards the product'), have remained fairly constant in their admiration, and need, for the monarchy over the years: in the latest poll, only 5 per cent thought Britain would be better off without the monarchy, while 63 per cent thought the country would be worse off. But of those 'ayes', there are differing classes of assent. At the bottom end of the scale, there are those users, who may not necessarily be choosers, but cannot escape the massive dosage served up by the media. There are those in the middle who respect the monarchy, and have a high, personal regard for the Queen (59 per cent at the last poll). Then there are the dedicated royal watchers, both professional and those loyal 'Palace gatherers': the professional cameras and the Kodak instamatics.

Amongst the last category, both amateur and professional, many regard the Princess of Wales and the Duchess of York as role models – that is as either leaders or trend-setters. Most of these are their exact contemporaries, or younger. Being former commoners, much of their appeal lies in the 'it could be me' syndrome. To some, the Princess of Wales is the epitome of some vicarious, fairy-tale dream. Amongst the progressive, there is the Duchess of York: Both, however, are the embodiment of 'myths for our time'.

Of the two, the Duchess of York's myth is straightforward: boy meets girl, girl meets *roué* and converts him, (not unlike the angelic girl in Max Beerbohm's *Happy Hypocrite* who converts Lord George Hell into Lord George Heaven and lives happily ever after). It is what every woman really wants, besides the converted *roué*, she has royal recognition *and* the freedom to enjoy it. By the same premise, the Princess of Wales, 'headhunted' *à la Princess and the Pea*, is the modern Cinderella: the 'rags and chores' after the arrival of Prince Charming, but before becoming Queen. Also, by fairy-tale law, it is Prince Charming, being the *only* one for the Princess, who stands for *permanence*: as opposed to the pop idol/hero who is purely transitory.

By their marriages, greatness was thrust upon them. They became super-stars overnight, they have fame and fortune, adulation and stardom, although the Princess of Wales's share is, of course, the greater. A large part of the worldwide success of them both is their share of, and performance within, the royal and non-royal 'princess market'. They start with a large initial advantage over all competitors being members of one of the oldest, and certainly the most respected, of the twenty-six monarchies in the world today.

These extant, and the many extinct, royal houses all have their princesses, but none remotely as acclaimed as these two. The majority of European foreign royal princesses are mere accessories; the bicycle princesses of Holland and Denmark, or the night-club princesses, Princesses Caroline and Stephanie of Monaco. The African and Arab (Moslem) princesses, in their thousands, are either enclosed in purdah, or from too poor a kingdom to have much effect. There are the princesses of other regal, and rich, royal houses, like Thailand and Brunei, but again, they are hardly comparable in style or effect.

Then there are 'domestic' members of the British Royal Family. The Princess Royal is a princess in a class of her own. Poacher turned gamekeeper, she uses her position as a Royal princess for the betterment of her charities, rather than for self-aggrandisement. Princess Margaret no longer captures the headlines, either good or bad, but works quietly away, while Princess Alexandra, with her endearing smile and charm, has always been acclaimed the 'nice princess'. Although not born royal, but nonetheless princesses, are the Duchess of Gloucester and the Duchess of Kent, both of whom keep a low profile, while her sister-in-law, Princess Michael of Kent, is somewhat of an acquired taste. The fringe royal princesses (although not actually princesses), like Lady Helen Windsor, Lady Sarah Armstrong-Jones and Marina Ogilvy all strive for, and generally achieve, anonymity, while Zara Phillips, Lady Davina, Lady Rose, and Lady Gabriella Windsor are all far too young to count. Nor will they ever. Others in the 'princess market' are the 'non-royal' princesses. These, women like Madonna, Vanessa Redgrave, Kiri Te Kanawa, Martina Navratalova, Winnie Mandela, Barbara Streisand, even Nancy Reagan are all successful and admired, not only in their particular field, but as women, or 'princesses', in their own right as well.

Such are the other princesses, or competition, in the market, yet none better represents the *ideal* princess (one who is virginal, dutiful, beautiful, uncriticisable, except for some controlled, or contrived, flaw that seems to make her human), more than the Princess of Wales. She has, of course, been 'relaunched' today as that glamorous, svelte, well-dressed mother of two. The same qualities are not quite attributable to the Duchess of York, but then her outward, ebullient, character, the Lady Bounciful approach, does have its own appeal, particularly in a market of changing tastes.

Today, through foresight and common sense, and with the help of a strong team of advisers, the Royal Family have found exactly the right level of exposure to the responsible media: neither too forward and open, nor too restricted and withdrawn. While only the odd, barely perceptible changes are now needed to keep this ancient and trusted monarchy up to date, there is still room for another, different approach on the periphery, so long as it still reflects the spirit, and retains the values of the core. This is what the younger members of the Royal Family (the Princess of Wales, the Duke and Duchess of York and Prince Edward), have to achieve. Their more liberal role and style, however, has been made easier for them by the 'middle-generation', the Prince of Wales and particularly the Princess Royal, having paved the way before. Just as the mantle of royalty has obviously changed the Princess of Wales and the Duchess of York, so they have put their mark on the Royal Family, not as an institution, but, in certain quarters, on the overall view of the monarchy.

To Work

Of all the Royal Family, only the sovereign has a specific role, and, even there, that role cannot always be clearly defined. As for the rest of the Royal Family, their *raison d'être* is to support the monarch. There are no set rules or jobs for any of them (a spell in one of the Services usually a branch of the Royal Navy), even less for the heir to the throne. The Prince of Wales has exactly the same problem as had all his predecessors: what to do as 'monarch-in-waiting'. There are no immediate guidelines or precedents for him to follow as to what he is supposed to do, or, frequently, not to do. It is entirely up to him as to what he does, and how hard he works. It is also up to him to decide how far he can, or cannot, go – he can be more outspoken than the Queen and Prince Philip, but less so than his younger brothers or his sister. What he has done, however, is to carve out for himself jobs in a sphere of national life which are basically non-political: conservation, the plight of the homeless and the like. Typically, he receives more media coverage from one controversial speech on the horrors of modern architecture, than all his work with the Prince's Trust.

After her wedding, the Princess of Wales was in exactly the same position, one of carving out an acceptable, public role for herself. There were, of course, plenty of offers from various charities, but she took her time. She began with a tour of Wales, the first of a lifetime of engagements. It was a huge success, her rapturous reception and popularity a great boost to her confidence. It was as if she had been doing it all her life. She was a natural. As the Duke of Edinburgh pointed out, there is no 'school for royalty', they just had to learn, 'like monkeys, watching and copying their parents'. But the Princess had no such training, yet she took to it with the greatest of ease. From the very first, she found that she had that great gift of spontaneous conversation (what some would call small talk): nothing very profound or remarkable, but exactly the right sentiment, for whoever. Her remarks, 'What nice shiny medals,' to an old soldier and 'Did you polish them for him?' to his wife, did more for her than any learned speech. As she became more self-assured, so she developed her art. The Queen Mother, too, has this rare gift of coming out with exactly the right remark in any situation, one that instantly allays any potential nervousness. Surprisingly, the Princess of Wales's voice is virtually accentless, without a trace of the Sloane Ranger's 'ra-ra' accent and words with clipped vowels.

From the very beginning, it is the Princess of Wales who invariably draws the huge crowds wherever she goes in the world. It must have made Prince Charles very proud, at least initially, to see the effect his wife had on them, even if it was at his expense. When on his own, a disappointed voice from in the crowd would ring out: 'Oi, Where's Lady Di?', to which he would reply 'She's not here. You'd better ask for your money back!'. When they are at some joint engagement on a 'walkabout' (an Australian Aboriginal term) the disappointment on the side of the street taken by Prince Charles is all too evident: 'I'm just the collector of flowers these days' is a common complaint as he receives bouquets destined for his wife, 'you'll have to make do with me.' During their visit to Germany in 1987, it was *Di und Charles*, leaving no doubt as to who was more important. An exact royal parallel is with the last Duke and Duchess of York (George VI

and the present Queen Elizabeth the Queen Mother). It was the
Smiling Duchess who the crowds flocked to see: in New Zealand,
they really did ask for their money back at a function she could
not attend through an attack of tonsillitis. In fact, so popular was
she, that when they arrived at a railway station, crowds would
run alongside their carriage, hoping for a glimpse of her. The
unnoticed Duke once jumped off the train to join the crowd
waving at her through the window!

Seven years into her lifetime 'job' with hundreds of engagements behind her, the Princess of Wales is now extremely
polished. She is far better on her own, than with her husband,
where naturally he takes precedence over her (she always walks
a few paces behind him) and makes the speeches – it is here, as a
doer rather than a spectator, that she often adopts that 'frightened
greyhound look', sometimes even going to sleep. Where she
excels, however, is at smaller, less formal gatherings, particularly
walkabouts, rather than the full-blown affairs, although she is
quite capable of handling even the most daunting on her own.

Launched young, and with an interest in children (can her job
as a helper at the Young England Nursery School and as a part-
time nanny ever be forgotten?), it was only natural that she would
gravitate towards charities that were child and youth-orientated.
To date, she is connected with 27 charities and organisations, in
varying degrees of involvement. Gone are the days when
members of the Royal Family accepted patronages of charities
and organisations like strings of brightly-coloured Hawaiian leis.
It is not enough to merely 'show the flag'. Instead, they only take
on these worthy causes where they can contribute something
more than a name. A prime example is the Princess Royal and
her work (among many other charities) with the Save the Children
Fund and Riding for the Disabled. With both, her knowledge of
the subjects is unrivalled. She knows what is going on, first
hand, through innumerable visits, both in Britain and abroad.
Knowledge gained from one is useful with another – at the
tropical diseases faculty at London University, of which she is
Chancellor, she can glean information and ideas for the field, just

as she can pass on her practical knowledge to the college. Above all, she cares, deeply. Hers is definitely a hard act to follow.

Like her sister-in-law, but not yet with the same recognition nor to the same extent, the Princess of Wales has become totally involved with her special charities. When she became Royal Patron of the British Deaf Association she learned the deaf and dumb alphabet to communicate with the handicapped: an attractive and appreciated gesture that showed immediate involvement. Only after three years as president of Dr Barnardo's was it revealed just how much she does for her charity. 'Her efforts belie the image many people have of her', the proverbial spokesman said, 'We have a very hard-working president. She is not just a figurehead. That in itself would be marvellous, but she has approached her role completely differently.'[1] She would turn up, unannounced, at their headquarters in the East End, to attend management meetings. She would join in on all discussions, particularly those on child abuse. Her behind the scenes work took her to families with disturbed, maladjusted and disabled children. She became involved with their work in placing teenagers and children who had been in care for some time into foster homes, a potentially difficult transition. On one occasion, visiting one such unsettled child in a foster home, the fourteen-year-old came home from school to find the Princess waiting for her, with a bunch of flowers. The child was naturally astonished and delighted, the flowers brought because 'she was always being given flowers and thought it would be fun to give some back'.

The staff at Dr Barnardo's also revealed that the Princess was 'very good at talking to young people. . . . She is able to relate to disturbed youngsters particularly well. It really is a morale booster to them and their families.'[2] Here she can certainly draw on experience of her own. Although only six at the time of her parents' separation, but hardly deprived, she well knows the anguish of the children of separated parents. The value of such work, until the press exposed it, was that it was done quietly, without fuss or publicity.

The material advantage to any charity or organisation favoured by a Royal presence is great. When that presence is a popular, hard-working member of the Royal Family, especially the Princess Royal, the Princess of Wales and the Duchess of York, then the advantages are seemingly limitless. With their support, it is obviously easier for the charity to raise funds, especially through organising some function or just through straight donations. One particularly lucrative seam for a charity is to have an evening, a ball, a concert or suchlike, sponsored by a company. As a business, members of the Royal Family cannot be seen supporting them, it would be tantamount to advertising and be unfair on their competitors. If, however, they underwrite a charity event, that is pay all the expenses leaving the profit for the charity, then a member of the Royal Family can attend. Everyone is happy, the charity has the money, the company the exposure.

Of the hundreds of such events annually, the ball held in September 1987 to mark one hundred and fifty years of the jewellers, Tiffany and Co., is typical. They approached the Duchess of York's lady-in-waiting, Helen Hughes, and invited the Duchess to the ball, asking her to name which charity she would like to benefit from the evening. She accepted, and named the Action Research for Crippled Children (she is Patron of the National Fund for Research into Crippling Diseases). The ball was organised by Tiffany's staff and a small committee. They would, doubtless, have sold all the tickets anyway, but having the Duchess of York associated with the event gave it an added dimension, and made 'more of the evening'. The ball was held at Sion House, Twickenham, just outside London. The Duchess arrived quietly and was ushered into a separate room to meet a few of the more important guests – mostly those connected with the organising committee, the company, and the charity. When the guests were all seated in the marquee for dinner, the Duchess discreetly slipped into her place, with no ceremony or fuss, amongst the 500 or so guests. After dinner, there was an auction of some earrings and a bracelet by Paloma Piccasso, some Tiffany's antique silver, and a small, Halcyon Days enamel box, donated by the Duchess, the lid decorated with her initial over a coronet.

The ball raised £40,000 for Action Research and, through the programme, made the guests aware of this organisation's work. The guests enjoyed the evening, if not actually meeting the Duchess at least 'rubbing shoulders' with 'royalty'. The Duchess enjoyed herself too, rising to the occasion by wearing a Tiffany blue skirt. For the sponsors, Tiffany's, the reward was even greater. The ball received the widest coverage in the press, far more, and indeed cheaper and much more subtle, than if they had taken out full page advertisements. Everyone was delighted.

Some advantages of Royal patronage of a charity are purely practical. They are never short, at least for long, of volunteeer workers, even if they join for all the wrong reasons. They all know well what a call from Buckingham Palace can do to overcome any logistical problem, or cut through red tape. Best of all, is the publicity and added coverage from the media: all that free adver tising and exposure of the cause. If the cause is in any way topical, like child abuse or Aids, then the Royal involvement has double the effect.

The Princess of Wales is a woman in touch with her times; an age and generation where alcoholism, juvenile delinquency and drug abuse are no respecters of background, class or money. She has an individual style that people can relate to, particularly the young and the very old, just as she can relate to them. The Prince of Wales has the same dedicated commitment to the young and old alike, possibly even stronger through his own varied works and trusts, but he does not have anything like the same, extraordinary charisma of his wife. With more 'clout', he may achieve more, but it is she who leaves the lasting impression. She simply shows that she cares. Her visits to hospitals, old people's homes, drug and alcohol centres and the like are undeniably stimulating, both for the patients and herself alike.

The Royal Family have, after all, always given succour to the afflicted: a visit to a major disaster area, a comforting telegram, a personal letter that means so much. It is all part of that role of the monarchy as a symbol of national unity. When they visit the scene of some disaster, the survivors, or attend a memorial service, they are not only showing their own personal concern, but acting as the people's representatives as well. It is the 'caring face of monarchy', seen so often: the Queen's visit to Aberfan in 1966 when a slag heap engulfed a school, or the Princess of Wales attending the memorial service for the victims of the King's Cross fire. Their concern also highlights the tragedy, like the visits of Prince Charles and Princess Diana to the flood victims in Wales, or their trip to Northern Ireland to talk to the survivors and relatives of the dead after the IRA bombing in Enniskillen on Remembrance Day. There, the sister of the youngest bomb victim said of their visit, 'It has really helped us. It was lovely to know that they care; hopefully, if this has affected the Royal Family, some good may come of it'.

The effect of a visit by the Princess of Wales on patients can be truly remarkable, one doctor going so far as to say 'magical'. A consultant at the National Hospital for Nervous Diseases said:

> She has a miraculous effect on people. There is an aura about her which has an enormous spin-off effect in terms of morale. Lots of these patients here have drab existences at home because of their condition. They become socially isolated. An event like this is something they never forget. Morale and happiness has an effect on the whole body. The uplift that the Princess gives them can sometimes do more than any doctor.

At a visit to open the new wing at the Middlesex Hospital, she shook hands with all nine, homosexual Aids sufferers. She sat on the edge of their beds and discussed their lives and problems at length. The photograph of the Princess shaking hands, *sans* gloves, with an Aids victim did much for her kudos; it did even more for the whole cause of all Aids' sufferers. That one, compassionate photograph, said more about the transmission of the disease, than hours of television commercials, posters and explanatory leaflets.

The royal touch has always been significant. The flight of James II in 1689 effectively put an end to the official belief in the divine right of kings (although 35 per cent of those polled in the late 1950s actually thought the Queen was appointed by God). With that divine right, the monarch was supposedly embodied with the power of healing, in particular scrofula, a hideous, disfiguring disease. 'Touching for the King's Evil' to cure the disease was common right up to the last Stuart monarch, Queen Anne. The Sovereign still kisses hands on the appointment of ambassadors, both to and from the Court of St James. Today, each member of the Royal Family approaches the business of shaking hands in an entirely different way, although one very much in keeping with their performance in public. Where the Queen keeps her hands firmly clasped round a bunch of flowers or the Duke of Edinburgh has his hands behind his back, the younger members of the family seem to launch into a crowd shaking hands with all and sundry. The Prince and Princess of Wales are inveterate hand-shakers on a walkabout; Prince Charles even acquiescing to the frequent demands to kiss him. The Duchess of York's style too, is typical of her approach: clasping banks of outstretched hands in a fit of enthusiasm.

Again, that effervescence and enthusiasm of the Duchess of York is typical of her approach to her role. Where she can be as dignified as any member of the Royal Family, for example at the Cenotaph for Remembrance Day, the more usual image of her is of the wide, flashing smile and rolling eyes, topped with that mane of red hair. She will pick up babies like a politician; dance with children as if at an end-of-term concert at a nursery school, and smile obligingly for photographers, like the Queen Mother. She can be boisterous too: her antics at one dinner in Canada were typical. Possibly because it was with the relaxed and egalitarian Canadians that they both felt that they could behave as they did, more likely they did not think at all. The Duke of York began making the speech, then handed over to his wife, who, after some jokey aside, pretended to strangle him. There were many who thought their behaviour unseemly, but, in the main, everyone loved this public 'horseplay', particularly the Canadians. It is impossible even to conjure up a picture of 'Di *und* Charles' behaving in the same way on their visit to Germany. What is good for the goose is certainly not good for the gander.

Like her sister-in-law, the Duchess of York has started slowly in creating her own 'portfolio' of special charities. So far, the Duchess of York has not yet developed a strong theme to her patronages, a modest list of eleven patronages that includes the patronage of The National Association of Flower Arrangement Societies of Great Britain, the Blue Cross Animal Welfare Society and the Combined Services Winter Sports Association. However, she is Grand President of the Royal Commonwealth Society. As Queen Elizabeth the Queen Mother is now less active abroad, it is likely that this is where the Duchess's forte lies. She was popular on her first trip to Canada, where her effervescent style went down well with the Canadians. Doubless, the Australians would warm to her too as did the Americans.

Again, public life is so much easier for the Duchess of York than for the Princess of Wales. Unlike Prince Charles, the Duke of York does have a real career as a lieutenant in the Royal Navy. As a serving officer, he is not expected to take on much of a public role, though many would say that he could do more if he so wished. His first duty is to the Service. As with every other newly married couple, the Duchess of York's first duty should be to her husband. Just as the Queen, as Princess Elizabeth, when first married to a serving Naval officer, the Duke of Edinburgh, spent as much time as she could with him on Malta where he was stationed, so the Duchess of York spent much time at her home, Chideock Manor, a rented house in Dorset, not far from Portland, where he was based.

In a television poll in December 1987, two out of three of those asked thought that the younger members of the Royal Family should have a conventional job. Apart from the Armed Services and the Foreign Office, there are, in fact, very few opportunities open to them. Everything with a possible political bias is out, as is anything where there could be a scandal, like a job in the City. A job at the criminal bar would have its obvious pitfalls. Industry is one area which would benefit from a royal presence. Prince Edward has opted for a job in the theatre, joining Andrew Lloyd

Webber's Really Useful Company as an assistant producer. The Duchess of York kept on her old job as an editor for a Swiss-based publishing company specialising in art books. Despite popular opinion, such jobs outside the Services and the Foreign Office for those younger members of the Royal Family are really a nonsense. How can Prince Edward start at the bottom of a career in the theatre, making tea and being a general dogs-body, when as a Prince of the Royal Blood he is being guarded by a detective? It can only be royal schizophrenia at its worst: Eddy by day, Your Royal Highness by night. Although the Duchess of York has now given up her job, that can not have been easy either. Publishing is all about meetings and conferences and people. With her office in Buckingham Palace, for obvious security reasons, how could she operate?

What these younger members of the Royal Family should be doing is to 'show the flag'. They are the 'limbs' of the monarchy, and as such, they should not try to be like everyone else. Their value is that they are all very different, and as such, embodied with a unique power to serve others. Taking an 'ordinary' job, besides being dispiriting for them, is merely depriving someone else of that job. To work for the public good, in whatever capacity, can only be advantageous to all parties.

6

Cinderella Goes to the Ball

To all but those very few who see the Princess of Wales and the Duchess of York in person, virtually the only view that is beamed round the world by the media is of what they, especially the Princess, are wearing, and how they look. It is their fashion, their hairstyles and their figures which excite more than what they actually do, or say. This is no criticism of them, apart from on those occasions where they actually court the camera and publicity, but of the media for portraying them almost exclusively in that light. Apart from weddings, no one comments on what the Princess Royal, who can 'make a bush shirt look like a regal cloak',[1] is wearing, who the designer was, or who did her hair. Instead, it is enough to report what she says or does, particularly if it is at some distant field hospital in an outlandish country. No one comments on the cut of the Duke of Edinburgh's or the Prince of Wales's clothes, unless he is wearing something totally unsuitable, like the staid, double-breasted suit he wore to the Band Aid rock concert. But for the Princess of Wales, who is continually adding to her wardrobe, it is one way of expressing herself, and her mood. In fact, it is also her one way of censuring photographers. She well knows that they can not sell photographs of her wearing clothes that have been seen dozens of times before, so when cross with them, out come the old numbers. No new clothes, no photographs and definitely no fee. For the Duchess of York, her attire is of less importance. With her sister-in-law's head start of six years, not to say sartorial inclination and superior income, she can never hope to compete. Instead, it is her actions that speak the volumes, and occasionally her words.

Naturally, it is all part of their role as members of the Royal Family to be perfectly dressed and presented. No one, ever, lets them down, and nor should they with valets, ladies' maids and hairdressers with them at all times. They all know what photographers will do to them if they notice even a loose button, a dropped hem or a ruffled skirt. When they spied the Princess of Wales's wrinkled tights, they called it her 'Nora Batty look', after a character in the BBC comedy, *Last of the Summer Wine*. Being perfectly dressed is also a question of good manners: during the Second World War, the Queen, the present Queen Mother, always put on her smartest clothes when she visited the bomb damage in the East End. 'After all,' she said, 'they put on their best clothes to see me, so I should do the same to see them.'

That the Princess of Wales and her fashion have become almost interchangeable, one with the other, fits neatly into the pattern of things. While the Royal Family are more closely associated with grandeur, tradition, pageantry, chivalry, and such like, it was the Princess of Wales, from the outset, who has represented glamour. Glamour, with a capital 'G' however, fits the public bill, but not the way the Royal Family like to be seen (glamour and glitter is for soap operas, while decorum is for the monarchy). Again, the Queen Mother, as Queen, provides another example. On a State visit to France in 1938, her entire wardrobe was copied from the Winterhalter portraits at Buckingham Palace: regal and striking without being theatrical. Also, in the 1930s, dresses were generally plain so as to show off the jewellery. Today's dresses are more ornate to make up for the lack of jewellery – except for some of the Royal Family who favour both. Unlike the other members of the Royal Family whose sartorial lead appears to come from *Country Life* or the *Field*, the Princess of Wales, with her model figure and legion, fashion plate looks, is straight from the pages of *Vogue*.

The transformation in her clothes is synonymous with her own rapid transmogrification: from a limited, typical Sloane Ranger wardrobe to the Hollywood-style, glitzy wardrobe that earned her the sobriquet *Dynasty Di*. In fact, the change began almost immediately she came into the 'public domain' with 'that dress': the shape of things to come, from David and Elizabeth Emanuel. 'That dress' was strapless, of black silk taffeta and pure romance. Although it caused a great stir at the time, it was little different from the one the Queen, when Princess Elizabeth, wore for the announcement of her engagement in 1947. From then on, it was merely a question of finding her style, and building up a group of designers sympathetic to her taste and her needs. It is no accident, however, that whenever she appears in public, whatever she is wearing, her attire is striking.

For a start, the Princess of Wales wears her clothes well, and clothes invariably look good on her, even those that are, occasionally, totally unsuitable for the occasion. Latest of those disasters was the tight, black leather mini-skirt and lace stockings that she wore to see the musical, *The Phantom of the Opera*, which owed more to a set in *East Enders* than Kensington Palace. Shopping, particularly for clothes, is one of her major enjoyments, and not just in expensive, luxury shops either. There has been much criticism of the alleged fortunes she spends on clothes. True, to be that well dressed does cost a great deal of money (but nothing like the figures bandied about in the press). In common with the rest of the Royal Family, the Princess is frugal: dresses are altered; collars added, changed or removed; colours changed. Contrary to belief, the Royal Family do not accept dresses free, however much the couture house would like to donate them for advertisement. She is passionately interested in clothes and fashion, relishing the hours she spends with her favourite team of designers. Now, full of confidence, she has shed her advisers or at least their advice, and makes up her own mind. Nor is she afraid to experiment, not always a great success, but the result is nonetheless different or striking.

Since the very beginning, the Princess of Wales has been an indefatigable, walking emissary for the British fashion industry, both at home and abroad. With only a handful of exceptions, she will always wear British-made clothes.

> She is one of the most fashion-conscious women in the world. When she popularised her romantic look which fitted in so well with her engagement and wedding, she was really following London fashion. Now our fashion has become sleeker and more sophisticated, the Princess has changed with it. She always dresses British and everywhere she goes people know this.[2]

Apart from all being *British* fashion houses (even if the designers themselves are not actually British), they all have one thing in common: a deep loyalty to their royal clients, and total discretion. While royal patronage has never done any of them any harm, they do not advertise it (quite the reverse, in fact, as those who sought to capitalise on it found a distinct cooling of royal interest). Most are embarrassed if a royal client is seen carrying one of their personalised bags in public, although today, the designers' names are not the secret they were.

While this image of 'the clothes horse for the British fashion industry' is naturally good for the industry, rewarding for the individual designers, there is a danger of it masking the 'horse'. Of late, her more outré designer clothes have covered more than her perfect figure, (a figure honed by hours of swimming, aerobics and dance), they have overshadowed her personality too. The Princess of Wales expresses herself in one of the best ways she knows: through her clothes. As a self-confessed avid reader of her own press reports, she can gauge the impact she makes, and alters her wardrobe accordingly. During the visit to Italy in 1985, she could see how her muted wardrobe paled in comparison with the sharp Italians. A few months later on her visit to the United States, she chose a remarkable wardrobe, one that would stand out in a crowd: slinky gowns in strong colours, brilliant red or graphic black and white. Finding that 'dressing for the camera' had the desired affect, she carried on in that vein. However, her high profile wardrobe put her in the ranks of a top fashion model or film star: a glamorous ambassadress for *haute couture* rather than an ambassadress of the monarchy. But that is not to say that she did not wear these clothes to the greatest effect. For her, fashion works both ways, to express herself and to safely rebel. Where that unsuitable black leather mini-skirt and those lacey stockings looked merely common, her new-style, platinum blonde hair and a peacock blue, rock 'n' roll suit with a bootlace tie was 'sensationally pop'.

Consciously or subconsciously, this surfeit of publicity and film-star image has finally told on her. At the Epsom Derby in June 1987, she was actually wolf-whistled as she crossed the paddock with the Queen, hitherto something that was unthinkable to happen to a member of the Royal Family. It put her in the transitory ranks of the 'non-royal' princesses (as opposed to that permanence of the perfect princess). Her clothes are now considerably toned down, more regal. That said, she is not above coming out with something totally striking when the critics have accused her of being dowdy, like that white, slim-fitting, one-shouldered evening dress, in a beaded material from the Japanese designer, Hachi, that she first wore in Australia, or the puff-ball skirt worn on a visit to Toulouse, France.

The Princess of Wales has always dressed for an occasion, particularly abroad. It is, of course, a form of tribute, not to say flattering, for a host country if a guest like either of the sisters-in-law goes out of her way to please. It is also a form of reflected glory for the host nation, when, say, the Princess of Wales wears a 'magical, silk evening dress spun from moonbeams, printed with Moorish crescents and moons' specially created for a visit to Spain. The national colours of Wales (green and red), and Canada (red and white), featured in the Princess's outfits when she visited the two countries, a detail noticed and approved by everyone. For the Duchess's visit to Canada, she even went one stage further and wore a (clashing) red maple leaf in her hair. Such little details are easy to bring off, and give so much pleasure. It may have been a coincidence, but the red of her Yves Saint Laurent outfit she wore for a visit to the Red Arrows Aerobatic team exactly matched their overalls. It was no coincidence, however, when the skirt of her evening dress was the unmistakable Tiffany blue at the ball to mark their 150th anniversary.

Sartorially, the Duchess of York has come a long way since her disastrous beginning. Those early dresses she chose for Royal Ascot shortly before her wedding, with wide hoops and bands, did little to disguise her then 'well-rounded figure' (in fact quite the reverse). That horizontally banded evening dress she chose for her pre-wedding photographs did even less for her. From there, the only way to go was upwards. She once told reporters in an unguarded moment that she would have 'to polish up a bit' on her figure (reputed 39–29–43). She lost pounds, and trimmed her figure through exercise and the swimming pool at Buckingham Palace. She then approached a number of designers, among them Yves St Laurent, the Paris-based couturier, whom she asked to come up with a few, serviceable outfits for both day and evening. The effect was instant and remarkable.

Saint Laurent is, of course, a French fashion house, and having so famous an English client is a considerable coup. As her sister-in-law had plumbed most of the British designers, she naturally had to go abroad if she did not want to end up dressing as her twin. That said, they are frequently seen wearing the same clothes – not hand-me-downs, but one friend passing on some fashion find to another. After all, one British ambassadress of fashion is surely enough. Such was the sartorial transformation and success of the Duchess of York that the popular press, predictably, invented a sartorial rivalry between the sisters-in-law.

The story is, of course, pure fabrication. The Duchess of York will never have the same fashion-plate looks or the figure as the Princess of Wales; her attributes lie elsewhere. Nor does she have the same dress allowance that the Princess of Wales can command. The Duke of York, as second son, receives £86,500 a year from the Civil List, plus his Naval Lieutenant's salary of around £18,000 (before tax). Such an income would appear adequate enough for most young married couples, but the Duke and Duchess do have many expenses to meet out of it. There are the houses, complete with staff, that they have to rent until their own house near Ascot is built. He shares two secretaries with his brother, Prince Edward, while her lady-in-waiting, Helen Hughes, is salaried. Then there is the entertaining which does not leave much for the Duchess to spend on a necessary wardrobe, where a single dress could cost £8,000. It is strongly rumoured that the Queen does give her a dress allowance to make ends meet. The Princess of Wales, on the other hand, is married to an extremely rich man. He does not draw anything from the Civil List, his income, around £1 million per annum, being derived from the Duchy of Cornwall.

Apart from their looks and the respective size of their dress allowances, the Princess of Wales and the Duchess of York could never be rivals, as what they require of their clothes, and what they want their clothes to do for them, is so totally different. Where the Princess of Wales uses her clothes to reflect her personality or current mood (often the rebel in her), the Duchess of York's natural exuberance virtually masks whatever she is wearing. On the face of it, her flying kit was purely practical. Yet when she received her wings and pilot's licence wearing her cream, polo-neck sweater and trousers, sheepskin jacket, flying boots and long, white scarf, her hair, plaited and kept in place by a pair of *diamanté* clips in the shape of biplanes, she carried it off as if it were the latest in 'aviation chic' – as she jumped down from the cockpit of her Piper Warrior, one witness was heard to exclaim, 'Crikey, it's Biggles!' There is a certain spontaneity in the way she wears her clothes, possibly brought on by the new-found thrill of dressing up as never before. Also, where the Princess has totally abandoned all semblance of her early wardrobe, that Sloane Ranger uniform, the Duchess of York has stuck faithfully to her original style, like the floral print dresses she feels so comfortable in.

Above: Aldaniti, the Grand National winner, and jockey on a sponsored ride through Windsor Great Park. She raised £3,000 for the Bob Champion Cancer Trust.

Prince Harry's first day at school, with an old boy, Prince William, and their parents.

Home ground: the Queen flanked by the Duke and Duchess of York in Windsor Great Park.

The Duchess active ...

... and the Princess passive.

Soap-opera glamour meets Royal glamour – the Princess of Wales and Joan Collins at a film première.

As a member of the Royal Family, every single gesture can be recorded. An ebullient Duchess of York, with her mother, Mrs Hector Barrantes, at Wimbledon.

Dubbed 'the motor show model', the Princess of Wales sitting on the bonnet of her husband's Aston Martin.

In the vain hope of losing the photographers during their skiing holiday, the Duchess of York livens up a dreary photocall.

Skittish behaviour caught by a photographer. Fun, but was it Royal?

'Big Red' in Canada. The 'action'
Duchess of York paddles a canoe on
her Canadian tour.

'In the mood' – as is now tradition, the
Prince and Princess of Wales start off
the dancing at a reception in Melbourne.

Drenched and happy – the Duke and Duchess of York at Niagara Falls, Canada, 1987.

The Princess of Wales visits a crocodile farm at Darwin, Australia, 1988.

Where the sisters-in-law have so much potential, it would be a dreadful waste if all that was remembered was what they were wearing.

The Family Matters

As the last car sweeps out of the George IV Gate each year, and travels down Castle Hill beside Windsor Castle, it marks the end of the Royal Family Christmas. The Queen, always keen to carry on any tradition of her father's, continued his practice of spending Christmas with the whole family at Sandringham, her private residence in Norfolk. Then, after the 'Royal baby boom' in the early 'sixties, Sandringham became too snug a fit for them all, and the Queen switched her Christmas house party to Windsor Castle. It is now a huge party of the whole family, cousins and second cousins, spouses and their children, the one time when they are all together in one, big, happy family.

As the Prince of Wales said (before his marriage), 'We happen to be a very close-knit family. I'm happier with my family at home than anywhere else.' It is, of course, because of who they are that they *have* to be a close-knit family. Part of the role of the monarchy is to provide a focus for national unity. If that focus itself is divided, then the role becomes meaningless. But, apart from the usual family squabbles, all appears well on the surface.

Where members of the Royal Family may not consider themselves very grand, they certainly live in a very grand manner. Not even the grandest and richest of the land-owning Dukes begins to compare with the Queen for style and richness. She has four major residences, Buckingham Palace, Windsor Castle, Sandringham and Balmoral, the major art collection of the world, and the servants and income to run these establishments. She also has the Royal Yacht, *Britannia*, paid for by the Royal Navy. The royal year, outside of their official duties, is marked in a traditional royal 'migration' between these castles and house, often HMY *Britannia* as well.

The Royal Family congregate at Windsor for the Easter holidays, then return there for the Royal Meeting at Ascot in June. The late summer, August and September, is spent in Scotland at Balmoral, sometimes starting with a cruise on the Royal Yacht around the Western Isles, stopping off to see Queen Elizabeth the Queen Mother at her Castle of Mey in Caithness, or the odd Bowes-Lyon relation on the way. Christmas is spent at Windsor, the New Year and most of January at Sandringham. Very often, Sandringham or Balmoral will be opened up at other times, to shoot or to fish, but then they usually use a smaller house on the estate – Wood Farm at Sandringham, Craigowan at Balmoral.

Once there, they are on holiday (apart from Ascot week), and the migration is very much an informal, family affair, relations and their guests coming and going throughout. That said, it is only at Christmas that her family do not have to make an appointment if they especially want to see the Queen. Each family has a London base. The Princess Royal, the Duke and Duchess of York and Prince Edward all have their rooms at Buckingham Palace, while in Kensington Palace (what the young Prince Charles called 'the aunterie'), are the apartments of Princess Margaret, the Duke and Duchess of Gloucester, Prince and Princess Michael of Kent and, of course, the Prince and Princess of Wales. Then, there are the State occasions and other official functions where the Royal Family all meet. Despite their own diverse ways throughout the year, the Royal Family tend to see more of each other, for longer periods, than most ordinary families. Not only are they a close-knit family, they are also intensely loyal too. When 'trouble comes, they close ranks'. At the time of Princess Margaret's breakdown of her marriage, the family rallied to her needs: the Princess Royal took over many of her engagements, she travelled in the Queen Mother's carriage for Trooping the Colour – nothing very significant in itself, but collectively the behaviour of a caring family.

Paradoxically, the Queen and Royal Family are undeniably different from her subjects (most of whom would have it no other way), but, at the same time, they are no different from them either. As the film *Royal Family* showed only too well, behind the grandeur and the mystique of Royalty, there is a perfectly ordinary, Christian, loving family. For example, there is many a subaltern from the Scottish regiments detailed to guard the Royal Family at Balmoral who, terrified to find himself sitting between the Queen and the Duke of Edinburgh, suddenly finds that it is no different to sitting between two close friends of his parents. That same paradox, of course, faced the two sisters-in-law when they married into the Royal Family. Becoming the daughter-in-law of the Queen, albeit a woman they had both known all their lives and a friend of their parents, was a great deal easier than becoming 'royal'.

Obviously at the outset of every marriage, there is that period of adjustment in the lives of both parties. In one way, that adjustment was easier for the Princess of Wales than her husband. She had exactly 'what she wanted', to quote her engagement interview: she was also very young, hardly with a developed lifestyle. She only had to cope with becoming royal. He, on the other hand, was a bachelor who greatly enjoyed his bachelor's life, decidedly set in his ways. Being born royal, he naturally knows no other life than being royal, its privileges, advantages and appalling disadvantages.

The adjustment to a life royal for the Princess of Wales was enormous, as if she were trapped by her new position. When the Queen Mother said on her own engagement in 1922 that she would never think again as she wished, she at least did not have to contend with television or prying photographers: (she did, in fact, once give an interview to the *Star* which sent the Household into a state of frenzy worthy of a Bateman cartoon). Princess Diana's life, particularly her marriage, is under continual public scrutiny. Every single gesture and action in public (both on duty and off) is 'news' – driving to buy winegums in the village shop, Prince Charles affectionately patting her bottom at a polo match, she sitting cross-legged on his Aston Martin 'like a motor show model' all become internationally 'important'. Such intrusions are no respecters of privacy, but are just part of the price she pays for her position and her popularity.

During their visit to Italy in 1984, the Prince and Princess of Wales went to an art gallery in Venice. Clearly enchanted by one particular picture, he was heard to exclaim to his wife, 'Wouldn't it be marvellous, darling, if we could come back one day soon with time to look at this on our own?' to which the Princess replied: 'But we never are alone, are we?'[1] As yet, they have still to return to see the picture, and if they ever do, they will still *never* be allowed to see it on their own.

For a start, wherever she goes outside, either shopping, or taking the children to school, she is always accompanied by an armed officer from Special Branch. Often, when she drives herself, she is followed by another car with armed detectives. Her two sons also have their own detectives, who sit in the back of the classroom (what a job!) of their day-schools. There are always policemen around, patrolling the grounds both at Kensington Palace and Highgrove, their Gloucestershire home.

The Royal Family function through their Households, who are either salaried, like the private secretaries or ladies-in-waiting, or supernumery (extra) ladies-in-waiting or equerries. Members of the Royal Family often make friends with members of their Households: the Dowager Lady Fermoy, the Princess of Wales's grandmother, is a Woman of the Bedchamber to the Queen Mother, Alexandra Lloyd, a childhood friend from Sandringham of the Princess of Wales is one of the Princess's ladies-in-waiting. Likewise, they make friends of their Household. Although the Prince and Princess of Wales's office is within St James's Palace there is constant movement between there, Kensington Palace and Highgrove. When they lunch or dine at home, there is generally at least one, often more of their Household there too. Added to that, there are the endless informal lunches or dinners connected with their charities and trusts; sometimes the colonel of one of their many regiments, or the teams of the Prince's many advisers. Tea in the nursery is the only sure escape for the Princess of Wales.

As an integral part of that Royal migration, there are those many weeks every year that the Princess of Wales spends with 'the in-laws', very much *en famille*, which, apart from Christmas, includes the Household and the constant tide of many guests that ebbs and flows. However, for her, going to Sandringham is, in a sense, like going home. There she can catch up with all her Norfolk chums, where once again, she is 'Miss Diana' to the local retainers. Recently, the Prince and Princess of Wales have taken over the Lodge at Balmoral where they stay, and so are out of the main-stream 'Castle-life' of that particular holiday. But despite this constant 'flood' of people that crowd her public and private life, she can feel alienated, even now, cut off from her former life, her own family and friends. Lonely in her ivory tower. Much of what makes the Royal Family different to 'what other mortals are' is that so much of their lives cannot be called their own. They are governed as much by outside influences as their own destiny. For the Princess of Wales, the price of her fame and fortune is to be 'swallowed' by the whole system – the Royal Family, their Households, advisers, et al.

In the early years of her marriage, it was the loss of her freedom that contributed to her sense of loneliness. The Princess of Wales has always been very close to her mother, Mrs Shand Kydd. But, although her mother does have a *pied à terre* in London, she divides most of her time between the Isle of Seil off the West Coast of Scotland and their sheep station in Australia: two remote and somewhat inaccessible places. Her father, Earl Spencer, although living in England, is somewhat out of touch since his stroke. Her younger brother, the raffish Lord Althorp, is working for NBC, the American network television company. The Princess is close to her sisters; Jane, her London neighbour is more accessible than Sarah who lives in Lincolnshire. Whereas the Princess felt that, inside, she was just the same person as before her marriage, the main core of her old friends felt inhibited or starstruck. As with all royal persons, making friends is always difficult: the genuine shy away in case they are thought pushy, the ingenuous push themselves forward. For instance, it was difficult, if not impossible, for friends like her former flatmates to drop in on her in Buckingham Palace 'after work', any more than she could just drop in on them. They can, of course, speak to her on the telephone by the hour. To meet, they had to be invited at a specific time, with all the pre-arrangements that took the spontaneity out of the relationship. She was once so lonely during one Balmoral sojourn that Prince Andrew even asked one of her former flatmates, Virginia Pitman, to stay.

Life was easier when they moved into Kensington Palace and Highgrove, she could ask her family and friends down for weekends.

Like women everywhere, much of their socialising is done through their children, and the Princess of Wales is no exception. Now that William has left his 'Dame School' (where Harry is now) to go to his pre-preparatory school, she at least meets other mothers with an interest in common, their children. She will go to children's tea-parties like the rest of them, but still she is the Princess of Wales (only the children take no special notice of her). In her efforts to bring her children up as 'normally' as possible, she takes them to school and joins in every parent activity. It must have been a proud moment for William when she won the mothers' race at sports day.

When the Prince of Wales was asked about the age-gap between him and his fiancée during their pre-wedding interview, he admitted that he:

> hadn't somehow thought about it. I mean it's only twelve years and lots of people have got married with that sort of age difference. I just feel you are as old as you think you are.

She certainly has had that effect on her husband, at least physically. Both are very fit and healthy. At forty, he is still the action man of his twenties, maybe not jumping out of aeroplanes or climbing mountains as much as he used to, but still playing high-goal polo, hunting in the winter, diving, skiing and keeping fit by jogging. However, as a married man, he has inevitably lost that glamorous, bachelor macho-image: the man always to be seen accompanied by a beautiful woman. Being sensitive and brought up virtually entirely with older people, he naturally gravitated to friends older than himself. Sir Laurens Van der Post now aged 82, William's godfather, is a prime example. Consequently he has always been older in thinking than his years. Initially, he responded to his younger wife's influence. There were all those little touches, her hairdresser cut his hair, or she sharpened him up sartorially, choosing his ties, persuading him to wear single-breasted suits as opposed to his usual more formal double-breasted. His valet, Stephen Barry, took it badly and resigned over her 'interference'. Others in his Household resigned over the changes after his marriages, but not necessarily to do with her.

The Princess of Wales, on the other hand, being less worldly wise, appeared even younger than her slender years. Initially, her interests were closer to life in her flat at Coleherne Court than the Palace – the care of children, jolly girls' dinners, trips to the local cinema, pop music, dance and shopping, none of which the Prince was remotely interested in. Obviously, their own children are a common source of pleasure, but the picture of the Princess eternally listening to pop music through her Sony Walkman, dancing and doing aerobics on her own is a solitary one. She has, in fact, been to infinitely more polo matches than ever he has to pop concerts. Whereas, contrary to reports, she quite enjoys watching polo, he dislikes the music and attends concerts, like Band Aid under protest or from a profound sense of duty. He is an opera buff and very knowledgeable, she prefers ballet.

The Prince of Wales has often said that he is a frustrated farmer (not an uncommon trait in the Royal Family). He is a true country man, both dedicated and knowledgeable: his friends are mostly drawn from the country. Like the rest of his family, he is never happier than when pottering round his own estates in the Duchy of Cornwall, especially his own farm at Highgrove, or dealing with any of the Royal Estates. He loves country pursuits. He hunts at every possible opportunity, and loves salmon fishing, at which he is an expert. He prefers riding in races than attending race meetings; somewhat bored by the social aspect of racing (at the Royal Meeting at Ascot, he will sneak off to play polo at the first opportunity). Gardening also gives him great pleasure. The gardens at Highgrove have been created by him, all the planning and much of his own manual work (as his bandaged thumb, split by a hammer when planting a tree showed only too painfully).

Once when visiting a distant neighbour's garden, his hostess asked him if the Princess was interested in gardening, to which he replied, 'No, she is still a little young'. The Princess of Wales was brought up in the country and, until she went to London was very much a country girl. After that, the country was a place to visit, for weekends or strictly limited periods (that said, she endures it longer for the sake of her children). She 'neither sows, nor reaps', nor does she enjoy 'country pursuits'. As a child, she fell off a pony, breaking her arm, which put her off horses. She has been astride a horse since but patently is neither amused by it, nor by equine conversation; Royal Ascot and a chance to gossip with old chums is much more her style. She can leave other sports royal, like fishing, stalking and shooting, quite happily to the rest of them, while for tennis, her particular forte, she finds few partners, opponents or interest within the Royal Family, least of all from her husband.

Given the choice, all the Royal Family (save for Princess Margaret) would prefer to live in the country. However, the Princess of Wales is still, basically, a typical 'Sloane-Ranger-mother-of-two'. Had she not married the Prince of Wales, she would doubtless have married to some worthy old-Etonian, ex-Scots Guardsman, now working in the City with a firm of merchant bankers, living in Chelsea, with an elder brother with an estate to go to for weekends. It would all be great fun – lots of shopping, Mediterranean holidays, skiing and amusing dinner parties, slipping into Annabels (the Berkeley Square night club) to dance until the early hours. Much of Royal life is tedious. A long dinner sitting next to a Japanese businessman who does not speak a word of English cannot be classed as fun, nor can visits to heavy engineering factories. Yet to those born royal they are all part of the 'job' – as Queen Mary said 'we are *never* bored visiting hospitals'. All hybrids revert to type in the end, and the Princess of Wales has, in her private life, subconsciously reverted to her 'Sloane' origins while Prince Charles has carried on in the only way he knows, a life Royal in the bosom of his family. That the Prince and Princess of Wales enjoy such wildly different lifestyles and venues in their own way, at their own times, is no reason for the press to suppose that their marriage is on the rocks. It is not unusual for husbands and wives to pursue different interests, especially when there is a twelve-year gap between them.

Initially, the Prince of Wales was proud of the worldwide popularity, and interest in his wife, then it became a source of irritation when it was made patently clear to him that it was she the crowds wanted to see and read about in the press. It can only have been irksome to him when he made a particularly poignant speech to see the only aspect reported was the length of his wife's skirt or her new hairstyle. As the Princess is so good on her own anyway, they now tend not to double up on engagements (unless for visits abroad or the odd evening engagement). Although they can do most of their engagements in the day, by car, train or an aircraft of the Queen's Flight, there are times when they are apart for several days. When they were apart for their sixth wedding anniversary (29 July 1987), on different engagements, it further prompted speculation in the press on the state of their marriage. 'Di ducks love night' as the *News of the World* had it.

The passion the Prince of Wales has for Balmoral is hardly shared by his wife. There she feels at her most trapped and lonely. So, amid mounting rumour on the state of her marriage, she left her husband to estate management, and returned to London with her children. This was tantamount to a divorce in every tabloid paper and magazine around the world. When there was no denial from the Press Office at Buckingham Palace, (how can they scotch a story based solely on conjecture?), it was tantamount to a confirmation.

As private individuals, the Prince and Princess of Wales should have, of course, the same rights of every individual to live entirely as they please. The popular press, however, thought otherwise. They reported the supposed breakdown in their marriage in the guise of looking at the constitutional position, where in reality their interest was prurient. What they failed to point out, or notice, was that they had been apart for the same length of time, six weeks, the previous year with no comment from them. It was just the same as with the Princess Royal, so frequently 'divorced' in the press (she once asked the editor of *Paris Match* soon after she was married if she was divorced yet). When Mark Phillips failed to turn up at Balmoral with her it was inevitably seen as the final breakdown of her marriage: that he was in the middle of harvest, the busiest time in the farming year, went un-noticed. However, the Prince and Princess of Wales could have taken the advice so freely offered and spent a little of that time together and so have avoided the fracas.

The public perceive the two marriages of the Prince and Princess of Wales and the Duke and Duchess of York in different lights. Where they want the Wales's marriage to work (as symbols of national unity it *has* to work, despite the conjecture served up by the popular press), they have no doubts that the Yorks' marriage is working. And so it should, for, on the face of it, the Duchess has virtually all the advantages over her sister-in-law.

For a start, the Duchess of York's husband is a far less complex character than his brother. He is not as clever as the Prince of Wales, nor is he beleagured by self-doubts. Prince Andrew's Mountbatten self-confidence takes him a long way. Where the Prince of Wales has developed a tried, tested and efficient routine with his Household and bachelor life, the only routine that Prince Andrew had was that directed by the Royal Navy and not by him himself. Also, being seven years younger than his brother when he himself married, he was consequently less set in his ways.

In many ways, the transformation from single to married, commoner to royal, for the Duchess of York was easier than for her sister-in-law. Being that much older, and having lived with a man before, married life held no surprises for her. Although popular right from the start, there was not the same clamour to see her as there was for the Princess. There was no Tour of Wales (a day-trip to York was hardly comparable), no important engagements expected of her in those early months. There were few demands on her time. Instead, she had the time to devote to her husband and set up their first home together, and to see family and friends.

She, like her husband, had many friends before they were married. Many of them came through her relationship with her former lover, Paddy MacNally, some of his were demimonde and show business stemming from his relationship with Koo Stark. Not unsurprisingly, many of these, and old school friends, have been dropped, and a whole new set of mutual, trusted, friends adopted. But this was all a gradual, weeding out process, not like the instant 'shock' treatment for the Princess. Nor has her relationship with any of her family suffered by her new, elevated position.

Her father, Major Ronald Ferguson, has been on the periphery of royal circles for decades; in the Army, as the Duke of Edinburgh's chum and now the Prince of Wales's polo manager. Where Earl Spencer is tucked away in Northamptonshire, now long retired from Court, Major Ferguson is always around at Windsor and in London, much in evidence and always accessible (judging by his numerous press interviews some would have it that he is too much in evidence). Where relations are not all they might be between the Countess Spencer and her stepdaughters, Susan Ferguson and her stepdaughter are great friends. The Duchess is also in close contact with her mother, Susan, now married to Hector Barrantes, a professional polo player. Although they live in the Argentine, mother and daughter do see each other from time to time, either in London or in the United States where they have a house.

Before his wedding, the Duke of York admitted that 'Sarah was mummy's choice originally'. It was indeed fortunate that the Queen approved so wholeheartedly of his choice. As the older and favoured son of the Queen's 'second' family, he has always enjoyed a far easier relationship with the Queen and the Duke of Edinburgh than has his brother, twelve years his senior. The Duchess enjoys that same, easy relationship with her mother-in-law, as indeed she does with the rest of the family: she is 'their kind of girl'. For a start, she makes the Queen's favourite son happy, and has given him direction in life. Taking him out of 'circulation' must also have endeared her. In many ways, she and the Queen are alike.

After the birth of the first baby, women divide into two camps – those who put their child first, and those who put their husbands first. The Princess of Wales clearly puts her children before her husband, while the Queen, undeniably the loving mother, has always put her husband before the children. The Duchess of York has seen, first-hand, what a roving eye can do to a marriage, and, such is their present relationship, there is no reason to suppose that the Duchess of York will not follow the Queen in keeping her husband foremost after the birth of their firstborn, an endearing trait in any daughter-in-law married to a favourite son.

A special bond has grown up between the Queen and the Duchess of York. They have much in common too. For one who has been brought up on an almost exclusive diet of the horse, particularly polo, they are well and truly 'in her blood'. Horse-talk is second nature to her. She rides well, and often accompanies the Queen when she rides out, often on one of the Queen Mother's retired steeplechasers, in Windsor Great Park, or wherever. Like the Duchess, the Queen married a serving lieutenant in the Royal Navy, so they have much to compare and contrast, then and now. Also of interest to the Queen was the Duchess's publishing venture of art books; the last being a collection of architectural drawings from the Royal Library at Windsor. Like most members of the Royal Family, they are both deeply interested in, and indeed practise, alternative medicine. Above all, the Queen enjoys her company and listens to her views.

> Those who meet the Queen regularly have noticed her habit of saying 'one of my young friends was telling me ...' They conclude that the 'young friend' is Sarah.[3]

Just being herself, lively, active and funny, the Duchess of York has slotted neatly into the Royal Family's pattern of life. Contrary to their public image, they are neither earnest nor stuffy. She shares their own, finely-honed brand of in-castle humour — she is particularly good at 'the game', (rather like charades, the contestant acts out a title or well-known phrase, while the others have to guess what it is). She enjoys the 'Royal migration' at every level. Her suite of rooms within Buckingham Palace (Prince Charles's old ones) is part home for her; Windsor and its proximity to the polo ground of Smith's Lawn is her old stamping ground, while she enjoys the country life and entertainment of Sandringham and Balmoral, with its grouse moors.

The Princess of Wales and the Duchess of York have been friends, and close friends at that, for years. They have come to rely, and lean heavily, on each other which has only served to strengthen that bond between them. As total opposites, each complements the other, both in their private lives and, more recently, in public. As two commoners married into the Royal Family, they also need each other: not that theirs is a 'them and us' situation, but merely that they obviously face their new life of becoming royal in a different way than if they were born to it. They can unwind together. They can also share confidences in the sure knowledge that they will go no further. Although highly unlikely with their carefully selected inner core of friends and members of their Household, there is always that chance that in an unguarded moment a word at a dinner party will find its way into the gossip columns with all the ensuing embarrassment.

The presence of the Duchess of York within Royal circles has considerably brightened the Princess's life. They greatly enjoy each other's company and marked sense of humour. Whenever they are seen together, they are invariably smiling and laughing, like naughty schoolgirls. In private, they are masters of the practical joke, as when they dressed up as police women on the night of Prince Andrew's stag party. Together they jolly up photo-calls when skiing, pushing each other around in the snow (to the obvious disapproval of the Prince of Wales). It has even been suggested that the Duchess of York has led her sister-in-law astray. Headlines appeared like 'Diana Hits the Bottle, Boozy lunches at Palace with her pal Fergie', and how she introduced her to her 'raunchy, show biz' friends. Never having lived that kind of life before her marriage, it would be understandable if the Princess wished to experience it. She does, in fact, have a few friends from the entertainment world, but mostly connected with her charities. Nor does she care for alcohol. After the charge of drunkenness she took the unprecedented (and surprising) step of denying it when being granted the Freedom of the City of London at the luncheon at the Worshipful Company of Grocers:

> Contrary to recent reports in some of our more sensational Sunday newspapers, I have not been drinking and am not, I can assure you, about to become an alcoholic.

When the Duchess of York's own 'honeymoon period' from the press was over, she continued to enjoy a popularity of her own making. Their next step was to create a rivalry between the two sisters-in-law. The Princess of Wales has often admitted that she reads everything written about her, (surely a mistake) and is deeply upset by adverse criticism. Equally, she is heartened, possibly overmuch, when she reads of herself in glowing terms, or sees on television the impact that she can make. Such is that impact, that she has often been criticised for 'dressing for the camera', something more in keeping with the stars of Hollywood, who need the publicity to survive in their jungle. The Duchess of York's appeal is for herself, her Lady Bounciful approach, and what she does and says rather than what she is wearing (which is often, according to her father, 'a disaster'). There is, of course, room for both of them, each in their own particular way. There is no rivalry between them, *per se*, just healthy competition, and that no different from any other of the Royal Family.

Competition has not figured in the Princess's life as much as her sister-in-law's, their backgrounds being entirely different. The Fergusons are a fiercely competitive family, with competition between the two sisters, and a father who spends most of his life playing world-class polo. The Spencers had none of it, in fact quite the reverse. For example, her father is an excellent shot. Competition in Field Sports is ungentlemanly – you do not try to shoot more or better than anyone else and, if you do, then you keep quiet about it. As a child from a broken home, the young Lady Diana was allowed to give up easily when anything became too difficult. When she did not care to return to her finishing school in Switzerland, as her mother said 'just picking flowers', she was allowed to leave. Jobs lasted as long as they suited. However, everything changed when she married and duty was naturally put first – she also plays a highly competitive game of tennis. Thus, the impact that the Duchess of York makes being seen climbing out of a 'plane or helicopter about to be awarded her pilot's licence, or flashing stylishly down a black-ski run does not worry her. She is merely pleased for her friend. Not that she ever wishes to upstage her sister-in-law, but she knows that she will always lead, by nature of who she is and whom she is married to. Throughout their lives, the Duchess of York is destined to walk a little behind her friend, the future Queen.

On the Trail of the Commonwealth

The two royal visits of the Duke and Duchess of York to Canada in July 1987 and the Prince and Princess of Wales to Australia in January 1988 could not have been more different, yet they had one thing in common. They were both considered unqualified successes, but entirely in their own way. The Canadians loved the Duchess for being herself, open, unassuming and enthusiastic, while the Australians, always admirers of the Princess of Wales, enjoyed her visit, the glamour and the unexpected element she always brings to a Royal Tour. The nature of the two tours was also very different, the one superficial, the other deep.

The Yorks' visit to Canada was deliberately high-profile, low-key. The visit was designed to show off the Duchess to as many Canadians as possible, and to introduce her to the mysteries of the Royal Tour. On this occasion, official functions were kept to the barest minimum, and all possible controversial subjects and venues, like the French language issue or republicanism, edited out. It was designed as a jolly, and that was exactly what it was. And the Canadians loved her for it. The Prince and Princess of Wales's tour of Australia, on the other hand, was a serious affair as chief guests in the Australian bicentenary celebrations. In the months of planning before the tour, they made sure that it was not made up merely of civic receptions, and that as 'old hands' at the game (the Prince of Wales at least), they did not shirk potentially controversial subjects – the plight of the Aborigines, the homeless, children and drug addicts. But each pair was fêted in their own way.

It was fitting that the Duke and Duchess of York should arrive at Toronto for the start of their 25-day tour of Canada – Toronto was originally called York after George III's second son, Frederick Augustus, he of 'The Grand Old Duke of York' nursery rhyme fame. However, despite the historical ties, they were met by a mixed reception as they arrived at the Leicester B. Pearson Airport. The tour had been built up to 'Fergie Fever' pitch until the day of their arrival when the *Toronto Sun* launched into them both. They called her 'Big Red' and 'Rowdy Fergie' and called her 'a giggling disco queen who drinks too much', while he was labelled 'the Duke of Pork'. The *Toronto Star* said they were 'among the least admired of the Royal Family', calling her 'fat, frumpy and with a tarnished reputation'. While the sobriquets may not have been meant unkindly, the rest of the profiles were. It did not take long, however, for the newsmen to change their tune completely.

They were flattered by her choice of a two-piece scarlet outfit and a broad hat supporting a cheeky maple leaf. They loved the way her eyes popped like organ stops when she met her double during a walkabout: 'Do people say you look like me?' asked the Duchess. 'All the time' came the predictable reply. The crowds that flocked around them and lined their route made it obvious which one they wanted to see: the Duchess of York. So much so that the Duke even apologised that, 'As everybody's come to see Sarah, I'm sitting on the wrong side of the car all the time' (protocol demands that he sit on the 'kerb-side' as he, the senior of the two, has to precede his wife, and so get out of the car first). The tour was meant to establish the Duchess and in that it succeeded. The ambivalent press soon changed their headlines to 'Carry on Sarah' as 'she paddled her way into the hearts of the

Canadians'. The couple endeared themselves to press and public alike. 'No-one could have won the affection of the Canadian people as quickly as the Duchess has done', the media had to admit. Even the *Toronto Sun* changed its tack: 'Not only has the Duchess proved that red-heads have more fun, they share it with the people around them.' They threw themselves wholeheartedly into the tour with everything they had; they helped to paddle the historic birch canoe that took them to Thunder Bay, on the shore of Lake Superior. There, their reception was enthusiastic, but Thunder Bay lived up to its name and a ferocious hailstorm sent the revellers inside.

On and on they went, each event more popular than the last. The Duchess's easy manner and infectious good humour was just what the crowds wanted. She waved the compère away at an open air concert when he tried to remove a pop group from the stage to the delight of the teenage audience. The group played on to the deafening chants of 'Fergie, Fergie'. The evening ended with the Duke and Duchess singing 'Land of Hope and Glory' and the Canadian National Anthem, 'O Canada', somewhat reminiscent of the last night of the Proms. The 'fat, frumpy, disco queen' was now 'oh so slim – and those effervescent smiles'.

At the Government reception, the Minister of Finance, Michael Wilson, went so far as to compare 'Big Red' with Anne of Greengables (Canadian literature being light on red-heads), 'a high-spirited girl who got into all sorts of interesting predicaments when young – including accidentally dying her hair green long before punk was fashionable – who grew up into a charming and captivating young woman.' The Duchess blushed like a young bride.

The Duke had particularly asked that their tour, which spanned their first wedding anniversary, should include 'an element of romance' which, in Canadian terms, if not world terms, means the Niagara Falls. After opening a civic centre in Mississuaga, near Toronto (the one the Prince of Wales declined to open as he thought it too ugly), they were off sight-seeing. Their helicopter made a 'precautionary landing' on the way to Niagara (as its twin had done in practice), but they took it all in a day's 'work'. A Government spokesman claimed that they were in no danger as the Bell-Huey helicopter was perfectly safe being exactly the same one that the Pope had travelled in in 1984 – divine intervention. A vast crowd turned out to see them, as they posed in front of the Falls, and took photographs; they donned blue waterproofs and made a quick foray through the spray, standing on the top deck of the *Maid of the Mist*. They emerged drenched, 'Big Red's Titian locks dripping: they laughed, they giggled, they held hands to their own, the crowd's, and the 800-strong press corps – total delight.

The organisers of the royal tour were delighted too at the success of Duke and Duchess. Where a mere 7,000 turned out to see them arrive, the crowds multiplied like amoebas every time they appeared in public. Everywhere they went, they responded to the crowd's curiosity and warmth. They were even applauded as they took their places at the small church in Coburg, a town celebrating its 150th anniversary. They cheered them louder than the winner of Canada's premier race, the Queen's Plate, at the Woodbine racecourse. The Duke looked somewhat overdressed in his black morning coat, top hat and furled umbrella in a land of informalities, not so the Duchess in her pink and green summer dress with a large straw hat. She presented the cup to the same winning owner who had won the same race in 1979, that time receiving the cup from Queen Elizabeth the Queen Mother. The Queen Mother has a particular affinity with the Canadians, as they with her, and the similarity between these two royal ladies was not lost on them.

Their 'official engagements' relaxed when they went off to stay with friends for two days, where they water-skied and planned their mighty canoeing trip. Then it was on to Winnipeg, capital of Manitoba, the 'prairie province'. There they were given an official welcome and a hospital wing was found for them to open – as *The Times* correspondent put it, 'one of the weightier days of their Canadian tour'. The Royal band-wagon then raced across the prairies and up to Edmonton, Alberta, arriving on the evening of 22 July. The premier, Mr Don Getty, explained that as London was seven hours ahead, it was already 23 July, their first wedding anniversary. To mark the occasion, he presented them each with a thigh-length fur coat of grey beaver and light brown fox. The ensuing storm of protest was as predictable as it was vociferous. The Household claimed that the gifts were 'a total surprise' and could not have been turned down without causing offence. The RSPCA and animal rights groups had a field day criticising the Canadian Government for putting their guests in an embarrassing position and through it, canvassing their cause, while the premier replied that the fur was farmed and merely representative of a major business of the region. Had the Duchess been more experienced in such matters, she would merely have taken the fur, thanked for it and passed it onto an aide and into oblivion. Instead, in keeping with her ebullient character, she had to try it on, showing it off with a whirl, without a thought of the consequences. The only lasting effect to her was that her husband cancelled the full-length mink coat he had ordered in Toronto as a surprise anniversary present for fear of inciting further protest.

The animal rights lobbyists also complained when they attended a rodeo and stampede at Medicine Hat: the use of wild horses they considered 'barbaric'. However, what the Duchess was wearing, a green Buffalo Bill, fringed, leather jacket with matching cowboy boots and a stetson, evidently was of more interest to the followers of the tour. The head of a huge buffalo was given to them, appropriately, at Head-Bashed-in-at-Buffalo-Jump. The Duchess named the hairy beast 'Andrew'. A more welcome present was a conical-shaped piece of gold from the manager of a gold mine in Yellowknife, in the North West Territories, the last venue of their official visit.

So the official, twelve-day 'Andrew and Sarah' show, as it was dubbed by the Canadian media, ended and their holiday could begin. Followed by a diminished press corps, they flew to a remote landing spot, romantically called Caribou Narrows, for the start of their 300-mile epic journey down the Hanbury and Thelon Rivers. The idea of having a press call was to discourage journalists from following the expedition. However, the hazards of the river, the insects and wild animals were enough to deter even the most ardent. For the Duchess, gone were the jewels and the designer dresses, and in their place were army fatigues, boots, a Davy Crocket racoon headband and a large Bowie knife at her belt. She was no less photogenic. Pulling on the fine-meshed hood, worn against the swarms of mosquitoes and the vicious black fly, called 'Rotar Rooters' by the Eskimos, they were ready. Watching the Duchess heaving a heavy backpack onto her shoulders with a 'Cor blimey', there can be few who could doubt the toughness of the woman. So they set off, led by David Thompson, who had taught Prince Andrew while an exchange student at Lakefield School, Ontario. For ten days they paddled east through barren country, hundreds of miles from civilisation. They camped on the river bank, 'in a different place to the grizzly bears' hoped the Duke, not to mention the equally dangerous brown, and black, bears and the wolves. Being summer, the bears are supposedly less hungry than in the depths of winter. Hungry bears or not, the expedition was still tough and an adventure. Before they left, Prince Andrew had stuck a label on their canoe 'Never underestimate the power of this woman'. Surely no one does any more.

As the Duchess of York cut a dash canoeing through whirling eddies of the rivers near the Arctic Circle in Canada, so the Princess of Wales cut an equal dash whirling round the dance floor in the heat of Melbourne, Australia, just five months later.

The first of three royal visitors during the bicentennial year, the Prince and Princess of Wales arrived in Sydney on 25 January 1988, two hundred years less a day after Captain Arthur Phillip landed with the first fleet made up of 1,000 assorted convicts and guards, the first European settlers in Australia. Even after the 25-hour flight, there was little time to catch up on the time-difference or energy, as they hurled themselves into the country's celebrations. Day one lasted for thirteen hours, the shape of things to come. Predictably, in a country with a strong republican element, there were demonstrations against their presence. The

Nobel Prize-winning author, Patrick White, branded them 'Royal Goons', while an Aborigine leader claimed that 'Charles, Diana and the Queen represent 200 years of oppression, subjugation and racism'.

Such criticism was indeed harsh. Not only is the Prince of Wales rather fond of the old radio programme, 'The Goons', but he is particularly sympathetic to the plight of the Aborigine. After a bicentennial concert, they went backstage where the actor, Jack Thompson, told him that 'after 200 years, the Australians are finding out what the Aborigines have known for 40,000 years'. The Prince replied: 'Well, I agree with you. Those are my sentiments entirely.' The Princess steered clear of the subject throughout the visit.

They were called 'The Chief Poms' of the day, and the Australians, through their own self-congratulatory euphoria, in the mainenjoyed their presence. But the presence of the Prince and Princess of Wales was an adjunct to the celebrations in Sydney, not the prime reason. They arrived by barge at the steps of the Opera House to officially launch Australia's day, one they referred to as marking 'their progress from convicts to capitalists'. The Princess sat, 'a wilting English rose' in the unaccustomed heat, as the Prince delivered his speech. Those of the reputed two million who descended on the capital and who may have heard it would not perhaps have agreed with his sentiments on the Aborigines, but the reports, as usual, were of the Princess and what she was wearing. 'Two new outfits in one day', they noted, one in white silk with a striped shawl, the other, a champagne-coloured lace and silk suit that 'brought wolf-whistles from the Sydney crowd'. So as not to miss anything of the excitement, she insisted on joining the premier, Mr Bob Hawke, on board the Royal Australian Navy frigate, *Cook*, to sail round the harbour, bursting with every kind of craft, large and small. The premier, who has long campaigned for a break with Britain, was clearly taken with his royal guests, the Princess in particular, going so far as a republican can in saying, 'She has the most beautiful eyes I have ever seen'. Later, they took the salute as 160 tall ships, led by

Britain's gift to Australia, the sail-training ship, *Young Endeavour*, sailed past.

Leaving Sydney to its post-celebration hang-over, the royal party moved on to Melbourne. Here, the Prince and Princess were fêted, warmly, as old friends. The city has one of the largest immigrant populations in Australia, with over a hundred nationalities; their itinerary little different from being at home, only in a warmer climate. They attended a multi-racial festival, admiring an acrobatic act by some Vietnamese boat people; they travelled up the Yarra River, landing and talking to the scores of people waiting in the sun to meet them. 'Give us a smile!' one man asked of the Princess. 'But I haven't stopped smiling all day,' she replied, which was true. Later, the Prince toured a slum district that was being transformed, while she rested for the ball that night held in their honour.

Yet again, anything that happens once in royal circles becomes a tradition. As the Prince of Wales said in his speech in Melbourne:

> Our lot, my wife and I, has been to start the dancing. I assure
> you, it makes the heart sink, to have to make an exhibition of
> ourselves. Now how many of you would like to try it?

And so they did. The Prince had asked the band to play Glenn Miller's 'In the Mood' and, taking his courage and his wife in hand, walked onto the dance floor. They began with a foxtrot, which slipped into a quickstep, and then veered into an energetic mixture of jive, boogie and rock 'n' roll. They flashed across the dance floor, the Princess whispering to her husband 'Steady, please slow down' as the pace hotted up. On and on they whirled, she pleading with the other guests to join them on the floor. They came on in droves when the band changed to another Miller number, 'American Patrol'. They were patently happy (despite their solo ordeal). She was at her most glamorous, her hair up in a French plait, wearing a strapless silk sheath, split to the left thigh in shell pink with large royal blue ink-spots. She sparkled in the sapphire and diamond pendant, earrings and bracelet, a wedding present from King Fahad of Saudi Arabia. The room flashed with cameras as bright as the fireworks the night before, and everyone loved it as much as if it were Terpsichore herself dancing.

Melbourne was in for another unexpected performance from the Princess the next day. They visited the Melbourne College of Music and dropped in on a cello class of eleven children, under the conductor, Henri Touzeau, playing Beethoven's Funeral March. The mischievous professor invited the Prince to play, but he declined having abandoned the cello years ago and recognising the potential exercise fraught with embarrassment. When the professor persisted saying that it would make a lovely photograph for the children, he knew he had the measure of him. The Prince then scraped a few, hideous notes out of the instrument, then the professor asked if the Princess would like to try. Striding across to a grand piano, she thundered out a few bars of Rachmaninov's Second Piano Concerto. The professor kissed her on the cheek, she blushed and ran from the room to a 'Well done' from her husband. The professor's verdict: 'She is a lovely, a very warm player. When I was standing beside her, I could feel the warmth from her body. She shows great musical ability and is very sensitive.' In the words of Mandy Rice-Davies, he would say that, wouldn't he.

Next stop was Adelaide where the temperature was over 100 degrees. More heat. More admirers. More hands to shake. People fainting in the waiting crowd. They travelled fifty miles along the oldest railway track in Australia by steam train, appropriately called the Duke of Edinburgh, to watch a paddle-boat race. At Goolwa, a holiday resort on the Murray River, as the Prince opened a museum and tourist development, she nearly fainted. Later, at a nursing home, she admitted that 'This heat's getting me down. I'm a real Pom about this sort of thing.' Not the most profound statement, but the *right* kind of remark that endears her to the public. At last an engagement in blessed shade, they visited the air-conditioned Gallery of South Australia to view the bicentennial exhibition of the Australian artist, Sidney Nolan. In the late afternoon, the Prince played polo on the ponies tried out by his polo manager, Major Ronald Ferguson, who always comes along for the ride.

Then it was back to Sydney for another hectic round of engagements. They travelled by boat, *The Solitude* (definitely misnamed on that day, as she was surrounded by a cacophony of small boats), to Terrigal Beach, fifty miles north of Sydney, for a surf carnival. The cooling breeze perked up the Princess who declared that she was taller than all the winning team of life-savers as she presented them with 'The Princess of Wales Plate'. At a visit to Darling Harbour, the Princess met someone claiming to be Kev the Koala Bear, who presented her with a boomerang 'to slap your two boys on the bottom if they misbehave'. The Princess, laughing, told him that she did not have to do that sort of thing, but accepted the boomerang anyway.

The Princess was absolutely in her element on their last night in Sydney at a fashion show in the Opera House. Billed as the largest fashion parade ever, Australia's Bicentenary Wool Collection gathered fifty-five of the world's top models to show off what nine international couturiers could do with their wool. The models pranced up and down the cat walk for three hours, the Prince of Wales momentarily nodded off, and all agreed that the star of the show was the Princess herself, neatly dressed in a Bruce Oldfield creation a royal blue, full-length dress with a double-breasted satin jacket.

No visit, anywhere, of the Princess of Wales is complete without something to do with children. She was equally in her element when visiting a Dr Barnardo's centre for children of broken homes. For twenty minutes she chatted with the children, and was monopolised by a girl called Trudy, who clambered all over her. The Princess, who had admitted that she missed her boys, loved it all.

Royal tours are planned months, if not years, in advance. The original plan was for the Prince and Princess of Wales to visit Fiji after Australia, but, when Fiji left the Commonwealth after a military coup, another venue had to be found. The King of Thailand solved their problem by inviting them there. As southern Australia had had more than its fair share of the royal guests, a visit to Darwin, capital of the Northern Territory, was not only fair but also a good break point on their onward journey. The country and the climate could hardly have been more different from the south, yet their welcome was as warm as the baking-hot day. Here, at an art gallery, the Prince had a better chance to meet the Aborigines – and to discuss their tenets of life, their ways, and their herbal cures. They responded to him, and were impressed by his knowledge. As the territory now made famous by the film *Crocodile Dundee*, it was virtually *de rigeur* that a visit to a crocodile farm be included in the tour. Crocodiles, all destined to become handbags, belts and 'croc-steaks', were kept firmly in their cages, save for the two the Princess was invited to 'stroke'. It cannot have been that exciting, but it made yet another photograph to be flashed around the world.

So the Bicentennial Royal Tour ended with a snap, and the visit to Thailand began. There, they were met by the Crown Prince and Princess Maja. No one who saw the two crown princes together, roughly the same age and the sons of comparatively young sovereigns, could not have recognised their joint problem, two kings-in-waiting. There was also the contrast of the two countries, the informality of Australia and the grandeur, and ceremony, of the King and Queen of Thailand's Court in Bangkok. At one the Princess was wolf-whistled, at the other the servants approached on their knees so as not to be taller than her when she was seated. Their tour took them to Chiang Mai, not far from where the Thai–Laos border war was raging – in an engagement only the day before, 200 of the enemy had been killed and a Thai jet fighter had been shot down by a Laotian ground-to-air missile. But that day they were safe as they took in tourist sights and a trip to a traditional umbrella factory, and of course another present. After a farewell dinner with the governor of the province, they left in an RAF VC10. Prince Charles hopped off at Bahrain en route for a few days safari with friends in Tanzania, while the Princess went all the way home to her children, and a full diary of engagements.

To compare the Duchess of York's trip to Canada and the Princess of Wales's visit to Australia like for like is hardly fair. It was the Duchess's first visit to Canada where she enjoyed a considerable novelty success. That she failed to live up to the silliest reputation put about before her arrival considerably enhanced her appeal. The Princess, on the other hand, has been to Australia many times before (her first visit as Princess of Wales in 1983 was an unparalleled, personal success). Although those Australians who care are not blasé about her, she is not the 'first-timer' she was. In a *Woman's Own* poll on the most popular Briton abroad of 1987, in Australia she has slipped from her number one position she had held for years, to number three, behind the Queen Mother and the Queen. Perhaps Australia was feeling her age.

Just as the Duchess of York was a novelty to the Canadians, so Canada was new to her. It proved a new challenge to her and she was determined to make it work. Married just a year, and without children, her life was still without a set routine. The Princess, seven years married and a busy mother, has a definite pattern to her life and, however enjoyable a trip like hers to Australia was, it is still unsettling and unhinges that pattern. Although parted from her children for just twelve days, she missed them dreadfully.

The nature of the two trips was also very different. Whereas the whole of the Canadian visit was designed specially to 'promote' the Duchess of York and to 'break her in' gently to foreign tours, the Prince and Princess of Wales were the guests of honour at a nationally important event. There was much more going on in the country than their visit. The content of the Duchess's tour was essentially lightweight, often little more than sight-seeing, without a hint of controversy, but it was just what the Canadians wanted. The Australia tour was hard, gruelling and well orchestrated to pack as much into the day as possible. Great stamina was needed just to keep going, with few opportunities to rest (the Yorks took days off between engagements to R and R, rest and recuperate). Nor did the weather help the Princess: outside in the sun the temperatures often reached over 100 degrees at the height of the Australian summer. The Duchess for her trip had perfect weather in July and August; even in the 'frozen north' by the Arctic Circle the temperature rose to 70 degrees, an average summer's day in England.

The role of both husbands of the sisters-in-law is also significant. Both go down well in the respective countries, not least as both can claim them as their *alma maters*, for a term or two anyway. There were still 'We love you Randy Andy' T-shirts around; the Prince of Wales was still being kissed by Australian matriarchs, though not by maidens, as in his bachelor days. The Duke of York always pushed his wife forward, referring to her constantly in his speeches or allowing her the last word. He is considerably less polished than his brother, and has nothing of his confidence, wit or control of the situation in public. Nor is he taken so seriously. Consequently, the Duchess is allowed to shine in the 'double act', while the Princess is overshadowed by her intellectually weightier husband. On such occasions, she can even look bored. That said, she is more memorable as a person than any speech her husband might make. Where the Yorks complement each other, the Waleses shine better individually.

However, both the Princess and the Duchess have that natural flair for dealing with people, for putting them at their ease, and coming up with exactly the right note. Both are extremely photogenic (when the Duchess is not rolling her eyes). They have been compared to Queen Elizabeth the Queen Mother, especially the Duchess of York, who has that knack of making everyone in a crowd think that they are looking at, or waving to them. They can work a crowd like buskers, plunging in so that everyone can share their presence. Also, their ordinariness is their strength. When one woman said of the Duke and Duchess in Canada, 'They're real royalty, but they're just like everyone,' she could have spoken for them all.

The success of the two royal tours is not easily measured in real terms. There were no trade delegations, cultural missions or the British Council in their wakes. But both tours reminded each host nation of their Anglo-origins, no mean feat in countries with a strong republican element. It warned them that once those links have been broken, they can never be restored. In those two visits, the sisters-in-law were flying the flag to the full for Britain, for the Commonwealth, and for the monarchy. But that is what they are there for.

Epilogue

The British monarchy is a unique institution, the envy of the world. No other country can boast anything remotely like it, nor begin to emulate that system that has evolved, steadily, for over a thousand years. As a system, it has produced a Head of State of Britain and the Commonwealth who is exactly right for the times – never more so than today, being neither too dominant or powerful like the elected presidents of America or France, nor grey and unassuming like the nominated presidents of Italy and Germany (the military rulers and despots are, of course, beyond comparison). However, over the last decade, the monarchy has been threatened, not by any deep, republican plot, but from those who, in purporting to support it, have been guilty of the steady trivialising of that most treasured possession.

It began two decades ago when, in a necessary effort to update the monarchy, the cameras were allowed behind the palace gates to film the Royal Family. The film had the desired effect, but had its drawbacks too. Thereafter, the monopoly of their privacy was broken and gone forever, and in its place came an unhealthy familiarity. As William Hazlitt wrote, 'Though familiarity may not breed contempt, it does take the edge off admiration.' With this new access, the British popular press began trivialising the

institution of monarchy as of their right, treating it as a mer-
etricious drama, the members of the Royal Family as a mere cast
of characters. When the Princess of Wales, and more recently the
Duchess of York, joined that 'cast', they were given star billing.
Naturally, the more they were portrayed as stars, the more they
were treated as such: the more they were given roles to play, the
more they had to play them, so as not to disappoint the 'audience',
something they cannot afford to do. There is even a new move
of clapping members of the Royal Family, as with the Duke and
Duchess of York, in church, something more reminiscent of
lightweight, theatre performances where the lead is applauded on
their first appearance. It is an ever-escalating situation. The
foreign press, however, are a law totally unto themselves. Where
a photograph of the Princess of Wales or the Duchess of York
makes for a front cover abroad, the Queen does not. And that is
the nub of the situation.

To much of the media, and their readers, the sisters-in-law are
becoming little more than entertainment value. It is true that a
part of the monarchy is pure entertainment. It is the pageantry
and the spectacle of a true royal occasion that thrills and excites
more than any stage performance ever can. But, if the monarchy
were to be reduced *solely* to that level, of mere entertainment
value, it would cease to have a point, and therefore be destroyed.
The institution of monarchy is above such things. Where an
audience may want, for a time, the musical 'Royalty' or the 'Fergie
and Di Show' with music by Andrew Lloyd Webber and produced
by Prince Edward, it is not what the monarchy is all about. Even
Lloyd Webber musicals cannot play forever with the same cast.

In a survey at the end of 1987, the public consensus was that
the young members of the Royal Family should be allowed the
freedom to live 'ordinary' lives. In the wake of the Prince of
Wales's speech on City architecture, they thought that the young
royals should be allowed to voice their opinions, even straying
into politics. 'Ordinary' jobs, even outside the Services, were
quite on the cards. However, at the time when Prince Edward
became an assistant producer with Andrew Lloyd Webber's the-

atrical group, The Really Useful Company, the Duchess of York resigned as the London representative of her Swiss-based publishing house. The only constraint seemed to be that old chestnut, cash: they should not cost too much. Apart from the Queen, all the Royal family are doing things that were unthinkable even ten years ago. They give interviews by the score, they appear on chat shows. They all dive into the crowds on 'walkabouts', some even allowing themselves to be kissed.

As in all areas of change, it takes time for a settled pattern to emerge. The monarchy is no different. In this latest period of change within the immediate Royal Family – the younger sons having grown up, the addition of the Princess of Wales and the Duchess of York to the 'family firm' – there are no precedents, no guidelines. There is that same, very real danger of going too far to appease public demand, as of not going far enough in the fear of becoming a slave to it. The popular press obviously encourages the former, being only interested in selling newspapers today, not in the state of the monarchy in the twenty-first century. With the sheer numbers of photographers and their sophisticated equipment, and the vigilance of the 'Rat Pack', it is only too easy for them to trivialise the younger royals. Often they bring it on themselves with skittish behaviour – the Princess of Wales and the Duchess of York in the Royal Enclosure poking a friend in the bottom with their umbrellas, or the Princess tweaking the President's braces on an official visit to Portugal. Neither Queen Mary, nor indeed Lord Mountbatten, would have been too thrilled to see her break a fake bottle (made of spun-sugar) over the Prince of Wales's head at some film studio, nor a girl squash a custard pie in his face. The media could not believe their luck. The public, in the main, enjoyed it. But was it *royal*?

The prime example of trivialisation came with the royal edition of the international television game *The Grand Knockout Tournament*, where teams of contestants are dressed up to compete in funny, slapstick games. This particular event, a medieval extravaganza, was held at Alton Towers, an amusement park in Staffordshire and masterminded entirely by Prince Edward. As a

production, it was faultless. It achieved all its aims to the full: to
raise money for charity, to be entertaining and to be fun for the
contestants. The Save the Children Fund, the World Wildlife
Fund, the International Year of Shelter for the Homeless and the
Duke of Edinburgh's Award all benefitted by £1 million between
them. The event was beamed around the world, and was generally
well received. The contestants, made up of stars from every sport
and from show business, patently had a wonderful time. Even
the four dukes called in as judges appeared to enjoy themselves.
The only contentious part of the whole event was that the four
teams were led by four of the Royal Family, the Duke and Duchess
of York, the Princess Royal and Prince Edward. The Princess of
Wales did not take part, not because such antics would have been
out of character, but yet another example of the licence extended
to her sister-in-law but denied to the future queen.

Although none of the team leaders actually took part in the
games, they were much in evidence. The Duchess of York led
her team from the fore, shouting like a cheer leader from an
American high school football match – 'B - L - U - E,' she yelled,
'the big, bad Blues', the name of her team. The two Princes were
not quite so vocal, but still much in evidence, playing to the
crowd and television cameras. Only the Princess Royal managed
to remain decorous, but at the same time being totally involved.
While the others shouted and cajoled noisily, hers was the 'strong,
silent team'. She clearly enjoyed the day, made a large amount of
money for the Save the Children Fund (her prime reason for
taking part in the first place), and came out of it with honour.
Not so her brothers and sister-in-law, whose conduct was later
criticised as trivialising the monarchy and bringing it into disre-
pute. There are no plans for a repeat.

The Princess Royal has best mastered what 'being royal' means
in today's terms. She works extremely hard, topping the list every
year for the number of engagements. Her commitment to her
many charities is total, being of real value, her knowledge of the
problems they face unsurpassed. She is highly respected worldwide in many spheres, not least as a member of the Olympic

Games Committee. She is intelligent and witty. Public opinion and press reports are beneath her. She is truly royal, yet unlike her sisters-in-law, she does not invite interest in herself or her family. What she does on the public and royal platform is enough to satisfy public need. To reach that position, however, has taken years of battle, with much speculation and innuendo on the way. She has achieved that difficult, almost impossible, balance of having the common touch while at the same time remaining fully royal.

The public (as opposed to the audience) look for both those qualities in the Princess of Wales and the Duchess of York. They want them to be endowed with the mystique of monarchy (such an overworked phrase) while, at the same time, to be the stars they have been *made* into. Like St Augustine, 'Let me be good, but not just yet,' they want to have their cake and to eat it; never an easy situation. In some ways, members of the Royal Family have become a form of substitute religion in what is now basically an irreligious society. Every civilisation has had its belief in a god, or gods. Where the Royal Family may not be worshipped like the Emperor of Japan (at least unofficially), they are invariably venerated and propitiated like gods by an atavistic public. For instance, wherever they go, they are given presents – the Princess of Wales's bamboo umbrella in Thailand, or the Duchess of York's buffalo head from Buffalo-Head-Smashed-In, to the mountains of bouquets and small presents on a walkabout. No one 'bunches' Princess Caroline of Monaco or Madonna in the street. Their 'images' appear everywhere, all round the world. Even in Burma, a photograph of the Princess of Wales was seen alongside Buddhist religious pieces in a family temple, each with its own candle. Those who meet the Royal Family put on their best clothes (as indeed do they), like going to church: being rude to a member of the Royal Family, in person, would be tantamount to blaspheming in church. They receive obeisance from 'mortals', just as they give fealty to senior 'gods'. Everything is as neat and tidy as can be for a Royal visit, as the Princess of Wales commented in Australia, 'There is always the smell of fresh paint wherever I go.' The Sovereign, though not actually appointed by God, is anointed with holy oil at the Coronation: but the monarchy transcends even such religious ceremony.

At the time of the abdication of Edward VIII, Stanley Baldwin coined the expression, 'The throne is greater than the man'. The Sovereign is only the incumbent for life of the institution, to do with it as he, or she, pleases. They have a sacred duty to that office, like owners of estates who see themselves not as owners, but as tenants for life with a clear duty to pass it onto the next generation intact, as they themselves inherited it. Only the Sovereign can change the style of monarchy to fit the times. The antics of two former Princes of Wales, Edward VII and his grandson, Edward VIII, had no influence on how the monarchy was perceived during the reigns of Queen Victoria and George V, largely due to a self-censoring press. Only when they became kings in their own right (albeit one for barely 12 months), did the monarchy adapt to their particular style. That said, there is no doubt that the Princess of Wales and the Duchess of York have changed the face of the monarchy *in the short term*, and then only *superficially*, through the popular press. In this decade governed by style, what they have done is to mirror the public *idea* of the modern face of royalty, *sans* trivia of course. Superficially, these sisters-in-law are more palatable for everyday consumption than, say, the sight of the Queen's personal standard flying from the flag-staff over Windsor Castle seen from the fast lane of the M4 motorway.

But the monarchy *is* the Queen. She has always been above such artificiality, her role too important to descend to mere 'soap-opera' levels. The Queen is respected as much as a head of State as for herself – the demonstrations of loyalty at her Silver Jubilee were proof of that. Her role as Head of the Commonwealth is more vital and crucial than even that of the Secretary General of the United Nations. Her influence goes far beyond political boundaries, where, as Walter Bagehot wrote over a century ago, she has 'the right to be consulted, the right to encourage, the right to warn' her Government. That same institution of the monarchy will be the legacy that, one day, she will hand down to the Prince of Wales, *intacta*.

But will it? Nothing that the Queen would ever do would debase the monarchy. Likewise, the Prince of Wales is a perfectly capable, hard-working and able man, well up to kingship when his time comes. He does his difficult, self-appointed job well, most of it behind the scenes. Yet outwardly, he is invariably cast in an absurd role that is not of his making, even less of his liking: his wife's milliner of more interest than his speeches. He is more often portrayed as some 'mystic nut' talking to his flowers, his visits to a croft in the Outer Hebrides or the desert with his 'tame guru' misconstrued, than as a capable and future king. If the former is the sole part he is given now, how can the same man suddenly be given another, responsible script when he becomes king? The monarchy and show business are, of course, totally incompatible. The one stands for permanence, the other can only be transitory. They are also contradictory. Where the monarchy stands as a core of national unity and stability, the entertainment world merely reflects the fashionable statement of the hour. Portraying the monarchy as such would be to replace a system that is unique and valuable, with something shallow and perfunctory.

And there lies the danger of what could too easily happen. The 'soap opera syndrome', hopefully, is only a transitory stage, while the fairy story analogy is much closer – things have to be bad before they can become good in the end, forever. In time, the public will be bored with a diet of 'royal super-stars'. They, the younger royals, in turn will not have to live up to an image that is not of their own making. When that happens, the Princess of Wales and the Duchess of York will become *truly* royal.

Appendix

PATRONAGES/PRESIDENCIES OF THE PRINCESS OF WALES

President	The Albany	Patron	Gloucestershire County Cricket Club
President	Dr Barnardo's		
Patron	Birthright	Patron	The Guinness Trust
Royal Patron	British Deaf Association	Patron	Help the Aged
Patron	British Lung Foundation	Patron	London City Ballet
Patron	British Red Cross Youth	Patron	The Malcolm Sargent Cancer Fund for Children
Patron	British Sports Association for the Disabled	Patron	National Children's Orchestra
Patron	The Commonwealth Society for the Deaf	Patron	The National Hospitals for Nervous Diseases

Patron	National Rubella Council	Patron	Royal College of Physicians and Surgeons of Glasgow
Patron	Northern Ireland Pre-school Play Groups Association (NIPPA)		
		Patron	Royal School for the Blind
Patron	Pre-school Playgroups Association – Wales – PPA – Cymru	Patron	Scottish Chamber Orchestra
		Patron	Swansea Festival of Music and the Arts
Patron	Pre-school Playgroups Association	Patron	Turning Point
		President	Wales Craft Council
President	Royal Academy of Music	Patron	Welsh National Opera Limited

PATRONAGES OF THE DUCHESS OF YORK

Royal Patron	The Tate Gallery Foundation	President	National Fund for Research into Crippling Diseases
President	Anastasia Trust for the Deaf		
		Patron	Chemical Dependency Centre
Patron	The National Association of Flower Arrangement Societies of G.B.	Patron	Combined Services Winter Sports Association
Patron	The Carr Gomm Society Limited	Patron	Search '88 Cancer Trust
Patron	The Dulwich Picture Gallery	Patron	Winchester Cathedral Trust
Patron	Blue Cross Animal Welfare Society	Grand President	Royal Commonwealth Society

Notes

CHAPTER 1

1 Penny Junor, *Diana, Princess of Wales*, London 1982
2 Brenda Polan, *The Guardian*, 30 July 1981
3 *ibid*
4 Sue Townsend, *The Secret Diaries of Adrian Mole aged 13¾*, London 1982, p. 96
5 Philip Howard *The Times*, 24 July 1987
6 Peregrine Worsthorne, *Sunday Telegraph*, 2 August 1981

CHAPTER 2

1 *Charles in his own words*, compiled by Rosemary York, London 1981
2 *ibid*
3 *ibid*
4 *The Daily Express*, July 1980

5 Philip Ziegler, *Mountbatten, the Official Biography*, London 1985 p. 21
6 Sue Arnold, *Vanity Fair*, January 1986
7 *ibid*

CHAPTER 3

1 Lady Cynthia Asquith quoted in John Pearson, *The Ultimate Family*, p. 32
2 Lord Napier to Theo Aronson, *Royal Family, Years of Transition*, London 1983, p. 237
3 Quoted in *The Ultimate Family*, John Pearson, London, 1968, p. 114
4 Philip Zeigler, *Crown and People*, London 1978, p. 130
5 John Grigg, Baron Altrincham, *The National and English Review*, August 1957

6 Robert Lacy, *Majesty*, London, 1977, p. 255

7 *Sunday Times* 2 January 1972 quoted in Lacy, p. 256

8 *Sunday Evening Post*, 19 October 1957, quoted in Lacy, p. 257

9 *Encounter*, October 1957, quoted in Lacy, p. 256

10 Pearson, p. 133

11 Lacy, p. 258

12 Quoted in Pearson, p. 167

13 *ibid*, p. 168

14 *ibid*, p. 167

15 Neilsen to John Pearson, pp. 174 and 175

16 *ibid*

17 Ziegler, p. 134

18 *ibid*, p. 136

19 Harold Nicolson, *Monarchy*, London, 1962, p. 303

20 Quoted in Pearson, p. 181

CHAPTER 4

1 Andrew Duncan, *The Reality of Monarchy*, London, p. 199

2 A. A. Milne, *The House at Pooh Corner*, London, 1928, pp. 123 and 124

3 Pearson, p. 199

4 *ibid*, p. 200

CHAPTER 5

1 *The Daily Telegraph*, 30 November 1987

2 *ibid*

CHAPTER 6

1 Suzy Menkes, *The Sunday Express Magazine*, July 1987

2 Davina Hammar, *Diana, Princess of Fashion*, London 1984, p. 9

CHAPTER 7

1 Georgina Howell, *Vanity Fair*, July 1987

2 *ibid*

Index